FRANCE AT WAR IN THE TWENTIETH CENTURY

Contemporary France
General Editor: Jolyon Howorth, University of Bath

Volume 1
   Humanity's Soldier: France and International Security, 1919–2001
   David Chuter

Volume 2
   The Road to War: France and Vietnam, 1944–1947
   Martin Shipway

Volume 3
   *France at War in the Twentieth Century: Propaganda, Myth
   and
   Metaphor*
   Edited by Valerie Holman and Deborah Kelly

To Come
   The Extreme Right Wing in France: From Boulanger to Le Pen
   Edited by Edward Arnold

   Recollections of France: The Past, Heritage and Memories
   Edited by Sarah Blowen, Marion Demossier and
   Jeanine Picard

   Party, Society and Government: Republican Democracy in France
   David Hanley

   The Shaping of French Environmental Policy
   Joseph Szarka

FRANCE AT WAR IN THE TWENTIETH CENTURY

Propaganda, Myth and Metaphor

Edited by
Valerie Holman and Debra Kelly

Berghahn Books
New York • Oxford

First published in 2000 by **Berghahn Books**

www.BerghahnBooks.com

©2000 Valerie Holman and Debra Kelly

Library of Congress Cataloging-in-Publication Data
France at war in the twentieth century : propaganda, myth, and
metaphor / editors : Valerie Holman, Deborah Kelly.
    p. cm. -- (Contemporary France : v. 3)
    Includes bibliographical references and index.
    ISBN 1-57181-701-8 (alk. paper). -- ISBN 1-57181-770-0 (pbk. : alk.
paper)
    1. France--History, Military--20th century.   2. Propaganda,
French--History--20th century.   I. Holman, Valerie.   II. Kelly, Debra.
III. Series: Contemporary France (Providence, R.I.) ; v. 3.
DC365.5.F73 2000
365'.00944'0904--dc21   99-35602
                                                       CIP

British Library Cataloguing in Publication Data

A catalogue record for this book is available
from the British Library.

Printed in the United Kingdom on acid-free paper

ISBN 1-57181-701-8 (hardback)
ISBN 1-57181-770-0 (paperback)

CONTENTS

List of Illustrations   vii

List of Contributors   viii

Editors' note on translation   x

Preface   xi

Acknowledgements   xii

Introduction   Myth and Metaphor: The Power of
     Propaganda in Twentieth-Century Warfare   1
     Valerie Holman and Debra Kelly

1. **From War to War: A Few Myths, 1914-1942**   15
    Annette Becker

2. **The *Marseillaise* as Myth and Metaphor:**
   The Transfer of Rouget de Lisle to the Invalides
   during the Great War   27
    Avner Ben-Amos

3. **The Image and Myth of the 'Fifth Column' during**
   the Two World Wars   49
    Christian Delporte

4. **Fighting Myth with Reality: the Fall of France,**
   Anglophobia and the BBC   65
    Martyn Cornick

5. **Pétain and de Gaulle: Making the Meanings of the**
   Occupation   88
    Christopher Flood

6. **Between Propaganda and Telling the Truth: The Underground French Press during The Occupation (1940-1944)**   111
   Olivier Wieviorka

7. **Heroes and Martyrs: The Changing Mythical Status of the French Army during the Indochinese War**   126
   Nicola Cooper

8 *A la recherche du soldat perdu*: **Myth, Metaphor and Memory in the French Cinema of the Algerian War**   142
   Philip Dine

Index   159

LIST OF ILLUSTRATIONS

Figure 1   Isidore Pils, 'Rouget de Lisle singing the
            Marseillaise for the first time in the house of
            Dietrick (*sic*), Mayor of Strasbourg'.
            Reproduced by permission of the Musée
            Historique de Strasbourg.   35

Figure 2   Jean Carlu, '*La Marseillaise*', November 1918.
            Collection du Musée d'Histoire Contemporaine –
            Bibliothèque de Documentation Internationale
            Contemporaine (BDIC). Copyright © Adagp,
            Paris, 1999.   36

Figure 3   George-Edward, 'Why not stick it up in the
            Chamber as well?', 1915   53

Figure 4   Poulbot, 'He was telephoning from the
            tobacconist's', 1916   54

Figure 5   Anonymous, 'This is Radio Munich...', 1939   58

Figure 6   The Britannia Monument at Boulogne, 1938   67

Figure 7   'Yesterday, Today, Tomorrow', 1942   74

Figure 8   General de Castries, *Paris Match* front cover,
            1954   137

Figure 9   Geneviève de Galard in nurse's uniform,
            Paris Match front cover, 1954   139

Figure 10   Geneviève de Galard loading wounded
            soldiers, *Paris Match* front cover, 1954   139

Figure 11   Geneviève de Galard in combats, *Paris Match*
            front cover, 1954   140

LIST OF CONTRIBUTORS

Dr. AVNER BEN-AMOS, Senior Lecturer in Education, Head of the Department of Educational Policy, School of Education, Tel-Aviv University. He has published studies on French civic education and collective memory. His book *Funerals, Politics and Memory in Modern France 1789-1996*, is forthcoming with Oxford University Press.

Professor ANNETTE BECKER, Professor of Contemporary History, Paris X Nanterre University; Visiting Professor at the University of Westminster. Agrégée d'histoire. Co-director of the Centre de Recherche de l'Histoire de la Grande Guerre (Péronne, Somme). Publications: *Les Monuments aux morts, mémoire de la Grande Guerre*, Paris, Errance, 1988; *La Guerre et la foi, de la mort à la mémoire 1914-1930*, Armand-Colin, Collection U., 1994 (English translation: *War and Faith, the Religious Imagination in France*, 1998, Berg); *Croire*, Historial de la Grande Guerre: Editions du CNDP (Collection Grande Guerre) 1996; *Oubliés de la Grande Guerre. Populations occupées, déportés civils, prisonniers de guerre. Humanitaire et culture de guerre*, Paris, Noêsis, 1998; *La Grande Guerre* (with Stéphane Audoin-Rouzeau), Gallimard-Découverte, 1998.

Dr. NICOLA COOPER currently lectures in French history, society and culture at the University of Bristol. She has published articles on French imperialism and on cultural representations of French Indochina, and her book entitled *France in Indochina: Colonial Encounters* will shortly be published with Berg.

Dr. MARTYN CORNICK, Reader in Contemporary French Studies, University of Birmingham. He is Editor of *Modern and Contemporary France*, and has published widely on aspects both of

French intellectual history (in particular on Jean Paulhan and the *Nouvelle Revue Française*) and Franco-British perceptions.

Professor CHRISTIAN DELPORTE, Professor of Contemporary History at the University of Versailles-Saint Quentin-en-Yvelines. Agrégé d'histoire; doctor at the Institut d'Etudes Politiques de Paris. Specialist in the political and cultural history of twentieth-century France. Researcher at the Centre d'Histoire Culturelle des Sociétés Contemporaines (UVSQ). Publications: *Les Crayons de la propagande. Dessinateurs de presse et dessin politique sous l'Occupation (1940-1944)*, Paris, CNRS-Editions, 1993; *Histoire du journalisme et des journalistes en France*, Paris, Presses Universitaires de France, 1995; *Intellectuels et politique au XXe siècle*, Paris-Florence, Casterman-GIUNTI, 1995; (avec Laurent Gervereau) *Trois Républiques vues par Cabrol et Sennep*, Paris, BDIC, 1996; *La IIIème République de Poincaré à Reynaud (1919-1940)*, Pygmalion-Gérard Watelet, 1998; *Les Journalistes en France. Naissance et construction d'une profession*, Seuil, 1999. Forthcoming: *Histoire de la Propagande en France de 1870 à nos jours* (Seuil).

Dr PHILIP DINE, Senior Lecturer in French, Department of European Studies, Loughborough University. Author of *Images of the Algerian War: French Fiction and Film, 1954-1992* (Oxford, Clarendon/OUP, 1994). Research interests: the economic, political, social and cultural restructuring of France since 1945, focusing especially on decolonisation; sport and leisure; and popular culture; with numerous publications in each of these fields.

Dr CHRISTOPHER FLOOD, Head of European Studies, University of Surrey. Author of *Pensée politique et imagination historique dans l'oeuvre de Paul Claudel* (1991) and *Political Myth: A Theoretical Introduction* (1996). He has co-edited *Political Ideologies in Contemporary France* (1997), *Currents in Contemporary French Intellectual Life* (in press) and two collections of essays on the politics of French intellectuals. He is co-editor of the "European Horizons" series for University of Nebraska Press.

Dr VALERIE HOLMAN, art historian, held the first GWACS Research Fellowship at the University of Westminster, 1995-97. She has since published on the history of aerial propaganda dropped over France in the Second World War, and on the history of twentieth-century art publishing.

Dr DEBRA KELLY, Senior Lecturer in French, University of Westminster; Director of the GWACS. Author of *Pierre Albert-Birot. A Poetics in Movement, a Poetics of Movement* (1997). She has published on writers and artists of the First and Second World Wars and is currently editing *Committing to Memory: Remembering and Representing the Experience of War in 20th-Century France.*

Dr OLIVIER WIEVIORKA, Senior Lecturer at the Ecole Normale Supérieure Fontenay-Saint-Cloud. Graduate of the ENS Fontenay-Saint-Cloud, agrégé d'histoire, his publications include *Les Libérations de la France* (with Jean-Pierre Azéma), La Martinière, 1993; *Nous entrerons dans la carrière. De la Résistance à l'exercice du pouvoir*, Seuil, 1994; *Une Certaine Idée de la Résistance. Défense de la France 1940-1949*, Seuil, 1995; *Vichy 1940-1944* (with J.P. Azéma), Perrin, 1997.

EDITORS' NOTE ON TRANSLATION

In order to make this book fully accessible to English-speaking readers, quotations from French sources have been translated. In all but two chapters only the English translation is given, with a reference to the original French source provided in the footnotes. The focus of Chapters Five and Seven, however, is the analysis of visual and verbal language, and therefore the original French is given for accuracy, with an English translation in the body of the text.

PREFACE

At the same time [as] the war was relying on inherited myth, it was generating new myth, and that myth is part of the fibre of our own lives.

    Paul Fussell, Preface, *The Great War and Modern Memory*

In 1995, the University of Westminster established a research group to study the relationships between conflict and culture in France during the twentieth century, from the beginning of the First World War to just after the end of the Algerian War. The Group for War and Culture Studies (France: 1914-1964) has a particular interest in the representation of war experience and its effect on the individual imagination, an approach which draws on the history of memory as well as the cultural artefacts through which it is sustained.

This book reflects both the wide-ranging interests of the Group, and its commitment to the fostering of interdisciplinary research by bringing together contributors who work in departments of modern languages, European and French studies, contemporary history, art history, and education. The combination of these diverse approaches, in individual chapters and across the book as a whole, reveals how propaganda is created, diffused and received, and the crucial role played in this process by myth and metaphor. Through theoretical analysis, historical example and the close reading of visual and verbal discourses, this book also analyses the effects of propaganda by considering its development, its forms and the ways in which it functions in the individual and the collective mind.

ACKNOWLEDGEMENTS

The editors would like to acknowledge the invaluable assistance of Helena Scott in the French Research Office at the University of Westminster. She combined a high level of professional expertise with unflagging good humour, and her dedication to the project made tight deadlines possible, and the book project a pleasure.

We are extremely grateful for the support given to us by colleagues at the University of Westminster, in particular Ethel Tolansky, Marie-Monique Huss and Hilary Footitt, and all the members of the Group for War and Culture Studies who have contributed to its research work.

We would also wish to acknowledge the financial support of the Service Culturel de l'Ambassade de France, and to thank in particular René Lacombe and Olivier Poivre d'Arvor, who have continued to show great interest in the work of the Group for War and Culture Studies.

Thanks also to Helen McPhail and Marlene Burt for their work on the chapters translated from French.

INTRODUCTION

Myth and Metaphor: The Power of Propaganda in Twentieth-Century Warfare

Valerie Holman and Debra Kelly

War and Culture

For thirty years between 1914 and 1964, France was at war. Despite Allied victories in 1918 and 1945, both the global and the colonial conflicts (Indochina and Algeria) in which France was successively engaged posed unprecedented challenges to her people, her territory and her status as a unified Republic and imperial power.

The Great War of 1914-18 was largely fought on French soil, leaving nearly one and a half million Frenchmen dead, four and a quarter million wounded, and countless civilians affected by the trauma of invasion, occupation and loss. It was, as Annette Becker points out in the opening chapter, a war in which no-one was spared. Devastation on this scale inevitably attenuated national pride, which was salved, as it had been in 1871 after the loss of Alsace-Lorraine in the Franco-Prussian War, by turning to colonial expansion, thereby setting in train a series of events that would ultimately lead to the debacles in Indochina and Algeria between 1945 and 1962. 'The colonial movement was at its height and France's Empire at its greatest extent just after the War; […] France proudly referred to herself as a nation of "100 million" (a figure that, because it included all the inhabitants of the colonies, effectively made France more populous than Germany). Furthermore, the victory of the Great War was seen as a vindication of French civilisation and as such provided the mandate for France's civilising mission abroad.'[1]

1. Kenneth E. Silver, *Esprit de Corps. The Art of the Parisian Avant-Garde and the First World War, 1914-1925*, Princeton University Press, 1989, pp. 259-60.

In the Second World War, the defeat of France in 1940 was followed by a humiliating German occupation, and rival claims to national leadership: the aging Marshal Pétain, who remained in Vichy, versus the relatively unknown and much younger General de Gaulle who from a base in London slowly rallied support from the French Empire, his compatriots in exile and ultimately Resistance groups inside France itself. Within six months of the Allied victory, France's first colonial war was fought – and lost – in Indochina between 1945 and 1954, and further colonial unrest led to the war in Algeria from 1954 to 1962, which effectively destroyed the official political discourse of a greater France uniting the *Métropole* (mainland France) with vast tracts of North Africa.

Forced to contend with defeat, depopulation and internal division, and continuously at war from 1939 to 1962, the French people were bombarded with propaganda, which, it will be argued, largely relied for its success on myths constructed around events, individuals and secret armies. Though mass communication came into its own in the First World War, there was no direct correlation between the increase in material and the amount of *factual* information either sought or produced for propaganda purposes. 'Paris during the War was so congested with myth, fiction, propaganda, prohibitions and proscriptions that the most basic realities of wartime life were, at best, only dimly perceived. [… Paintings] of war subjects in modernist style were extremely unpopular; the Parisian public preferred to see the war handled in the traditional manner, by artists… who confirmed its home-front mythologies of battle.'[2]

The preference for myth over reality applied both to so-called 'high art' and to popular prints such as *'images d'Epinal'*, woodcuts in the style of a French folk tradition originating in the sixteenth century, and reaching its apogee in the late nineteenth century. Adopted by numerous artists working in both world wars, this type of print 'bore the message of war enthusiasm in a direct and unadulterated way. Their very naivety and self-consciously child-like style had a dual effect; to mythologise the war and to announce the virtues of escape from a reality at times too harsh to bear. […] Time and again the mythical war was re-fought in this corner of the visual arts, as it was re-fought in posters, illustrations

2. Silver, pp. 81 and 85. See also Philippe Dagen, *Le Silence des peintres : les artistes face à la Grande Guerre*, Paris, Fayard, 1996, who contests this view, and argues that the rise of documentary photography *did* mean that 'the realities of wartime life' could be clearly perceived, while modernist paintings of the war were not so much unpopular as nonexistent.

and eventually in film. *Images d'Epinal* came to form an important part of the unofficial propaganda effort of France.'[3] Folk culture also played an important part in the Second World War, when, for example, official propaganda of the Vichy regime had frequent recourse to the discourse of the fairytale, whose themes and narrative techniques could be instantly apprehended.[4]

To understand how propaganda was designed to appeal to its audience, the authors represented here have turned their attention not to Modernist art and literature, but to just such sources of popular imagery and narrative, and also to songs, speeches and satire.

Where '*Paris/Paris, Créations en France 1937-1957*', the centrepiece of a great series of exhibitions held at the Pompidou Centre nearly twenty years ago, celebrated individual creativity, constant innovation, and the rich diversity of artists attracted to the French capital, more recent publications on the arts in France have in several cases echoed research in the social sciences and looked at manifestations of cultural life that would seem to indicate not so much a desire to break with the past as to retain a sense of continuity and traditional frames of reference.[5]

Writing about French thought, Tzvetan Todorov's definition of culture is particularly apposite here: 'Culture is a classification of the world that allows us to get our bearings in it more easily; it is the memory of the past that belongs to a community, which also

3. Jay Winter, *Sites of Memory, Sites of Mourning. The Great War in European Cultural History*, Cambridge University Press, 1995, p. 127.

4. See: Christian Faure, *Le Projet culturel de Vichy : folklore et révolution nationale, 1940-1944*, Presses Universitaires de Lyon: Editions du Centre National de la Recherche Scientifique, 1989.

5. Notable among such recent publications are Jay Winter's study of collective remembrance *Sites of Memory, Sites of Mourning: The Great War in European Cultural History*, Cambridge University Press, 1995; Kenneth E. Silver's *Esprit de corps. The Art of the Parisian Avant-Garde and the First World War, 1914-1925*, Princeton University Press, 1989, pp. 259-60, showing that despite appearances the avant-garde was deeply embedded in French society; Romy Golan's *Modernity and Nostalgia: Art and Politics in France between the Wars*, New Haven and London, Yale University Press, 1995, arguing that cultural retrenchment after the First World War lasted well into the 1940s, and Laurence Bertrand Dorléac's *L'Art de la défaite 1940-1944*, Paris, Seuil, 1993, which looks at a broad spectrum of the arts in Occupied France, and while focusing on the imaginative qualities of fear, hope and nostalgia, is careful to distinguish between true and false continuities in French culture, notably the traditions promoted by the Vichy regime. More broadly based is Raoul Girardet's *Mythes et Mythologies Politiques*, Paris, Seuil, 1986, which spans the last two hundred years and addresses four main themes, of which 'the Saviour' and 'Unity' are most relevant to the subject-matter of this book.

implies a code of behaviour in the present, and even a set of strategies for the future.'[6] It is with the aim of helping to reach a clearer understanding of the complex relationships between war and culture that this book has been compiled.

Propaganda

From 1622, when the Vatican established the *'sacra congregatio de propaganda fide'* (the Sacred Congregation for the Propagation of the Faith), a committee of cardinals in charge of foreign missions who were helping propagate the faith of the Roman Catholic Church, propaganda has often been associated with spreading the word to a mass audience, likely to be unbelievers in need of persuasion, and located far from the seat of power. This is, however, to identify only half of its significance. The implication is that initiators of propaganda *need* to gain the support of a particular mass audience to ensure their own survival or effective action.

It was during the First World War that propaganda was initially used as a weapon on a large scale, and its effectiveness closely observed by all the belligerents. One of the most significant lessons they learned was 'that public opinion could no longer be ignored as a determining factor in the formulation of government policies'.[7]

At a time when memory has become a legitimate field of study for historians, and emotions, beliefs and public opinion are, if not yet central, at least increasingly accepted adjuncts to the depiction and understanding of forces shaping events and the reactions to which they give rise, this book addresses the ways in which propaganda appeals to the imagination. Where memory functions in the present, but derives its *raison d'être* from past experience, propaganda – though frequently drawing on pre-existing rhetoric, myth or expectation – looks forward: its success depends on a correct reading of hopes and fears, and is measured by the extent to which its concrete form affects beliefs and actions yet to come. An effective example is Christian Delporte's chapter on the Fifth Column, in which he points out that since the time of the Dreyfus Affair, public opinion in France had been sensitive to questions of

6. Tzvetan Todorov, *On Human Diversity: Nationalism, Racism and Exoticism in French Thought*, Cambridge, Mass., Harvard University Press, 1993, p. 251.

7. M.L. Saunders and P.M. Taylor, *British Propaganda during the First World War 1914-1918*, London, Macmillan, 1982, p. 1.

espionage and treason, and this laid the ground for belief in a modern myth used as propaganda not just by the French, but by all participants in the Second World War.

Arguably the crucial period for determining the extent of propaganda's role in warfare was a rare period of peace: 1918-1939. The interwar years saw each major European power reflecting on its own and its neighbour's recent attitude towards propaganda, and the success or failure with which it had been handled. While the German army acknowledged that it had taken too little account of morale in the First World War, Adolf Hitler's conclusion was much more sweeping: 'It was the total failure of the whole German system of information that urged me to consider the problem of propaganda in a comprehensive way. The lack on our side was exploited by the enemy in such an efficient manner that one could say it showed itself as a real work of genius'.[8] The British Foreign Office, however, was by then concentrating on creating a favourable climate overseas, and was heavily influenced by an awareness that France spent more than any other nation on *cultural* propaganda.

By the outbreak of the Second World War, there were many different ideas as to who, in any country, constituted the audience for propaganda. A British publication of 1940 concluded that 'One thing [...] stands out in all the leading generalisations about the popular mind which the propagandists of dictator states have adopted and proclaimed, and this is an unshakable belief that people in the mass exhibit a childish, primitive, inferior, mean and altogether despicable intelligence.'[9] This was a view exemplified by Hitler, for whom it was not a means of instruction, but was designed to attract attention, to 'appeal to the feelings of the public rather than their reasoning powers.... In the field of propaganda, placid aesthetes and blasé intellectuals should never be allowed to take the lead'.[10]

---

8. Adolf Hitler, *Mein Kampf* (trans. and annot., James Murphy), London, New York, Melbourne, Hurst and Blackett Ltd, reset for this edition 1942, trans. 1939 (1924), p. 106. By 1933, it had sold more than one and a half million copies, but in 1940 it was banned in France by the Germans, who realised that when the official line was to promote collaboration between the two countries, a book which stated 'France is and will remain the implacable enemy of Germany' (p. 341) was both true and bad propaganda.

9. F.C Bartlett, *Political Propaganda*, Cambridge University Press, 1940, p. viii.

10. Hitler, *Mein Kampf*, p. 110.

In France and the U.K., however, the target audience tended to be not the undifferentiated popular mass beloved of dictatorships, but clearly specified groups. At the end of 1941, for instance, the British Minister of Economic Warfare and Labour politician, Hugh Dalton, wrote a paper expressing the view that British propaganda should be addressed to her best friends in Occupied Europe: the industrial workers. The Director General of the Political Warfare Executive, responsible for propaganda policy, commented to the Foreign Secretary: 'I think our propaganda is already based on the hypothesis that in the Occupied countries the broad masses have more of the stuff of resistance in them than the bourgeoisie.' The masses were not seen as malleable, but obdurate. In January 1942, a long memorandum to the Propaganda Policy Committee by the Regional Director for France agreed, and extended the list of target groups to include 'Professional, technical and intellectual classes, because... they are our best allies. The importance of the immediate influence and leadership of [these] classes is very considerable, and should not be overlooked'.[11]

As the range of potential media increased, so too did the sophistication with which it was used for propaganda purposes. From songs and posters, to the press, photographs, radio and film, no means of communication remained untouched by those who sought to convey at least a partial truth persuasively. Like many aspects of propaganda, the focus on a specific art-form or medium could backfire: some, such as photography after the war in Indochina, became seen as inherently less truthful because their very plausibility had led to over-use by propagandists.

The most devastating example of reaction against a too believable myth, as Annette Becker argues, must surely be the Holocaust. In the First World War, people were inundated with printed images and stories of atrocities that were subsequently proved to be, if not wholly false, in many cases at least highly exaggerated. How then, in the Second World War, could people who had been proved credulous be expected to believe new stories about the treatment of Jews?

Propaganda takes effect not just through what it says, but also through how it is disseminated and where it is received. Taking truth and propaganda as the two poles of his argument, Olivier Wieviorka focuses on the clandestine press in the Second World War, and looks at how the constraints imposed by censorship

11. Public Record Office, file FO 898/13.

made telling and accepting the truth a challenge. Paradoxically, distribution methods echoed those of propaganda, and had a similar effect: whether clandestine journals were openly handed out in the metro, or delivered by saturation coverage of selected districts, the manner in which they reached their readers created the impression, and hence contributed to the myth, of a strong and powerful Resistance.

The contributors to this book have explored not only propaganda as objects of historically specific material culture, but also what it reveals of how the propagandist envisaged his readership or audience, what conditioned his decisions on how best they could be reached, and what in fact was the final impact. Any analysis of how propaganda works must take into account who is saying what, to whom, when and where. Christian Delporte, for instance, discusses 'private' propaganda, posters advertising Ricard, and designed to be put up in a place of conviviality – a bar – yet carrying the slogan *'se taire, c'est servir'* (to keep quiet means to serve), a subtle warning of the potential presence of German spies, against whom the best defence is silence. Such examples show how essential it is to underpin any historical account with an awareness of how meanings are made, transmitted and received: attention to language and iconography is thus particularly important. Propaganda itself rapidly adopted the metaphorical language of mythmaking: it acquired a body ('the fifth arm'), a mind ('psychological warfare'), and by the Second World War, even came in two colours, 'black', or 'white'. That propaganda as an idea should be subject to the same dynamic of mythmaking as events and individuals, suggests a powerful need to embody metaphorically any force that represents either a major threat or the possibility of superior strength in wartime.

Myth

War itself provides one of the oldest illustrations of the process by which myths of origin can subsequently be adapted to suit the needs of other civilisations. Ares (Mars), by common consent among his peers the least popular god on Mount Olympus, represented to the Ancient Greeks not the virtues of heroism or even tactical superiority, but violence and brute strength. Castigated by his father Zeus for his obstinacy and lack of self-control, he was not invincible in battle as might have been expected, but on separate occasions lost two fights to a goddess, was wounded by a hero, and was taken captive by a pair of giants. That the personification of war should have been one of the first twelve deities in Greek mythology is perhaps less surprising than the character with which he was endowed. Unappealing rather than awesome, Ares, though physically strong, cut an almost absurd figure, and was rarely portrayed by the Greeks themselves. If his unattractive nature is seen as a counterbalance to his undoubted force, this suggests that from the outset resistance to, and repugnance for war, as opposed to the personal qualities of heroism and bravery it invariably occasioned, was built into the conceptualisation of conflict, allowing for a range of reactions. Under the Roman Empire, however, the figure of Mars was transformed. The god of war was given the highest honours at Rome after Jupiter, reflecting the Romans' exaltation of military power and glory. Similarly, in German mythology, Odin, oldest of the gods and supreme among them, is associated variously with battle, magic, inspiration and the dead, and it was during the Viking period that the war god took over many of the functions of the sky god. Odin, both father of the gods and father of the slain, adopted as his sons all the fallen champions of battle, brought back to Valhalla by the Valkyries.

As Robert Graves has pertinently remarked in his introduction to a popular history of mythology: 'Myths are seldom simple and never irresponsible'.[12] They stem from the need, whether of an individual or a social group, to account for the inexplicable, to express powerful emotion, to master fear, or to celebrate victory. Whether communicated visually or verbally, old narratives are passed on, updated, or even subverted, to accommodate the requirements of successive generations living under new regimes, experiencing new forms of combat, or seeking a figurehead as a focus of resistance. They can even suppress an unpalatable truth, as Martyn Cornick shows: when politically expedient, the myth of the Entente Cordiale was used to mask the reality of Franco-British discord.

Indeed, it is precisely the durability of ancient myths and their potential for continuous regeneration that has made them so fruitful not just as an alternative to present reality, but as a way of

---

12. Robert Graves, *Larousse Encyclopaedia of Mythology*, London, Paul Hamlyn, 1959, p. viii. Graves is particularly interesting, in that his autobiography *Goodbye to All That*, published in 1929, remains one of the classic testaments of war experience, while he is equally celebrated as a poet, translator, historical novelist and author of the first modern dictionary of Greek mythology.

incorporating or narrating selected elements of the past to support a particular argument. Exploring the relationship between culture and collective memory, the historian Robert Gildea asserts that 'what matters is myth, not in the sense of fiction, but in the sense of a construction of the past elaborated by a political community for its own ends'.[13] Christopher Flood's chapter shows exactly how this was done when he compares the competing claims to historical legitimacy as leaders of the French people made by Pétain and De Gaulle in the 1940s.[14] He also provides a perceptive analysis of mythopoeic political narratives.

Embodiment is a leitmotif throughout this book, for it represents an almost instinctive attempt to make believable the existence of a miraculous happening or invincible leader, or to bring within the compass of human imagination something as amorphous as the Fifth Column. It is no coincidence that during the Second World War de Gaulle and Pétain feature as 'symbol' and 'emblem' in d'Astier's 'dictionary of pseudonyms' used by the Resistance, nor that, as Nicola Cooper remarks, 'the myth of liberation [was] embodied in the choice of General Leclerc, liberator of Paris, as the first commanding officer to oversee the expeditionary forces in Indochina'. As vehicles for more generalised hope and aspiration, figures of myth or distant history such as Joan of Arc, Geneviève (the patron saint of Paris), and above all Marianne – the ever-changing incarnation of France – represented a counterbalance to contemporary heroes who acquired mythical status.[15]

The converse of embodiment is the space opened up by suppression of the real. Annette Becker explains why those experiencing the trauma of invasion and occupation in the Second World War could not learn from similar events in the First World War: such memories had been deliberately obliterated in a collective need to forget; Nicola Cooper argues that ambivalence in the relationship between France and Indochina caused this colonial war to be ignored in mainland France; Philip Dine discusses 'the war without a name' (Algeria) in terms of the most significant myth of all: the war's nonexistence. The suppression of reality,

13. Robert Gildea, *The Past in French History*, New Haven and London, Yale University Press, 1994, p. 12.

14. The mythical dimension is well handled by Ian Ousby in *Occupation: the Ordeal of France 1940-1944*, London, John Murray, 1997.

15. See for instance Maurice Agulhon, *Marianne into Battle: Republican Imagery and Symbolism in France, 1789-1880*, trans. Janet Lloyd, Cambridge University Press, 1981 (1979).

whether forgotten, ignored or refused a name, makes possible its replacement by a mythical entity more open to manipulation and more susceptible to representation for purposes of propaganda.

By considering propaganda not solely in terms of its artefacts but as an affective process in which artefacts play a determining role, and by analysing the language in which wartime propaganda is couched, the essays in this book focus not only on the importance of myth-creation, but on the rhetorical devices by which myths take hold.

The Metaphorical Process

Myths are therefore continuously being created, in order to make believable the unbelievable by harnessing the power of the human imagination. Hence the need here to attempt an analysis of how the processes by which such creations are given credence function. The forms which myths take in the extreme situation represented by war, and the ways in which they are diffused, is central to every chapter of this book. Inherent in all these various analyses is an attention to process, processes of creation and of propagation. Yet how do they function? How is a new meaning grafted onto an image, a memory, a person, an event? Why is such a transformation, such a shaping and reshaping permissible, and often readily acceptable? What appears to be happening is a shifting and displacement of meaning analogous to the metaphorical process. Although the analysis of the use of individual metaphors as a rhetorical device would be a valid field of inquiry for the understanding of myth creation and its use in propaganda, this is not entirely the perspective within which the contributions here work. As Paul Ricoeur has noted:

> … metaphor is the rhetorical process by which discourse unleashes the power that certain fictions have to redescribe reality. By linking fiction and redescription in this way, we restore the full depth of meaning to Aristotle's discovery in the *Poetics*, which was that the *poiêsis* of language arises out of the connection between *muthos* and *mimêsis*.[16]

16. Paul Ricoeur, *The Rule of Metaphor: Multi-disciplinary Studies in the Creation of Meaning in Language*. Trans. R. Czerny with Kathleen McLaughlin and John Castell, University of Toronto Press, 1977; London, Routledge and Kegan Paul, 1978; paperback edn, 1986, p. 7. Originally published in French as *La Métaphore vive*, Paris, Seuil, 1974, (p. 11).

Here a 'rhetorical process' is considered with regard to the ways in which such a 'redescription' of reality takes place, how such a power is liberated, and how the perception changes while the 'thing' – person, event, image, memory – remains the same in its essence. It can therefore be suggested that the mythmaking fundamental to propaganda actually functions in a 'poetic' way, in a process akin to the functioning of poetic metaphor. Roger Cardinal, in his analysis of the poetic function and the poetic imagination in his book *Figures of Reality*, puts forward the argument that in order 'to make sense of the strangeness transmitted by the poetic text, it becomes necessary for the reader to set aside his intellect and instead to consult the associative suggestions supplied by his low-level sensibility.'[17] This appeal to the imagination rather than to the intellect was already well understood by the creators of propaganda in the First World War, as we have seen in our earlier section. Olivier Wieviorka makes the precise point made here, that propaganda addresses the imagination, not the faculty of reason, 'by opening up a space to dream'. Cardinal continues by stressing:

> ... the importance of analogical thinking as an instrument in man's general quest for an intimate adjustment to his environment. Because the confrontation with verbal metaphor prompts us to marshal our non-rational associative faculties, poems may be said to sponsor fluency within our mental and sensory circuits, making us more alert to the ways in which the perceived world around us is shaped and reshaped.[18]

The functioning of metaphor demands a certain 'collusion' between the sender and the receiver for the message to convey meaning. In the case of propaganda this implies that the acceptance of 'myth', far from being an exercise in brainwashing the masses as it has sometimes superficially appeared to be, is rather a complex process in which the individual, and eventually the collective, 'allows', through the suspension of the rules of the rational mind, the displacement, even the usurping, of the original meaning, and a type of 'new' meaning to come into being. It is not a truly new meaning, but a transformed meaning which emerges and opens up new possibilities for the understanding of a message which may now function on different levels. Indeed,

17. Roger Cardinal, *Figures of Reality. A Perspective on the Poetic Imagination*, London, Croom Helm, 1981, p. 13.
18. Cardinal, ibid.

metaphor 'is not so much a change of meaning as an evocative exploitation of given meanings'.[19] In the construction of a myth, a construction which takes place at a threshold between the outside world and the inner world of the mind, the metaphorical process itself is at work. In the chapters which follow, Annette Becker shows how the myth of the 'barbarian invader' is the obvious recourse brought in to deal with the occupation of northern France in the First World War, and how this masks at a deeper level the guilt of being invaded. Avner Ben-Amos provides his own analysis of the way in which metaphor helps us structure our perception of the world by means of explaining one thing in terms of another, and goes on to show how the French Revolution and the successful wars which followed were used to render more intelligible the unknown, and therefore menacing, aspects of the First World War. Christian Delporte charts the development of the idea and 'forms' of the Fifth Column, described by one commentator he quotes as 'a Machiavellian octopus', a revealing use of metaphor combining fear of the hidden forces of nature with the sophistication of political manipulation, both equally dangerous; and he goes on to note how certain images used in propaganda 'continued to resonate in the French imagination'. Martyn Cornick presents Laval's propaganda rhetoric in which Britain, 'perfidious Albion', has led France 'to the bottom of the abyss', and refers to the discourse of the threat of the Bolshevik 'plague' being used as a weapon, as disease metaphors often are in propaganda; yet what also become clear in this chapter are the ways in which events such as Dunkirk, Mers el Kébir and Dakar are transformed in this 'metaphorical process'. In the clearest use of metaphor contained here, Nicola Cooper reveals the processes at work in the transformation of Dien Bien Phu into '*le Verdun tropical*' (the Verdun of the tropics), '*le Verdun de la brousse*' (the Verdun of the bush), '*le Verdun de la jungle*' (the Verdun of the jungle), and '*le Verdun tonkinois*' (the Verdun of Tonkin); defeat is transposed firstly into a celebration of the army which remains at its post in the face of overwhelming odds, and finally into heroic martyrdom. In the last chapter, coming full circle to the problem of dealing with guilt and trauma revealed by Annette Becker at the beginning of this book, Philip Dine analyses the filmic metaphors of the Algerian War and argues that individual confession, so frequently por-

---

19. F.C.T. Moore, 'On Taking Metaphor Literally', in David S. Miall (ed.), *Metaphor: Problems and Perspectives*, Brighton, The Harvester Press, 1982, p. 12.

trayed, is presented as a model for the collective catharsis of the French nation.

In order, finally, to illustrate with a very concrete example the rather abstract idea of the functioning of metaphor in the cognitive process, the following case study carried out by Roger Tourangeau is particularly revealing.[20] His research into how we understand metaphors involved creating metaphors about topics which were new to the reader. One group was given metaphors about characters and places which did not exist. The example which he used concerned a 'Donald Leavis', described as 'the George Wallace of Northern Ireland'. The name of George Wallace generally evokes for Americans a politician with a flamboyant personality, a troubled marital history and a controversial political philosophy. The characteristics attributed to him are those of being a Southerner, anti-Black and conservative. After receiving this metaphor about 'Leavis', it emerged that the group involved in the research thought of Leavis as a bigoted politician, as anti-Catholic rather than anti-Black, and as Conservative. Therefore while Wallace's conservatism was transferred directly to Leavis, since it was applicable in both political contexts, his racism was transposed to be consistent with its new domain. The results, therefore, showed how parallels are constructed between figures in different domains, and other metaphors used in the research showed that this was not particular to this one metaphor, but holds true generally. Tourangeau, using his own effective metaphor, comments on the choice of characteristics pertinent to the domain presented and 'the transformation and shifts in emphasis [which are] smuggled across the borders between the two realms.'[21]

Tourangeau also shows how metaphor depends on congruence and agreement between the domains presented in the metaphor. A metaphor is more likely to be accepted if there is a high level of both congruence and agreement, hence the recognition and immediate understanding in the case of one of the most effective metaphors in this collection, '*le Verdun tropical*'. If the transformation effected by metaphor is indeed 'smuggled across the borders between two realms', then in the case of propaganda, the contraband which is already familiar is more readily accepted.

---

20. Roger Tourangeau, 'Metaphor and Cognitive Structure' in Miall, pp. 28-29.
21. Tourangeau, ibid.

Conclusion

The essays which follow explore how and why propaganda was created and received during a period in which France was almost continuously affected by the experience of war: 1914-1964. Each author considers a different aspect of myth, and looks at the process of its construction, recycling, and in some cases demystification, charting a course analogous to the production and effect of metaphor, which is itself seen to play a crucial part in myth's credibility.

Successive chapters document an increasingly sophisticated response to the mass media, and bring out the often paradoxical results of using myth in propaganda. What initially proved to be an effective measure in time of war subsequently had a subtle but profound effect on how populations perceived the relationship between reality and representation, fact and falsehood. The myth-making that began as a means of sustaining belief in France's supremacy, and later her will to resist, ultimately proved counter-productive in the process of decolonisation.

1

FROM WAR TO WAR:

A Few Myths, 1914-1942

Annette Becker

Between 1914 and 1918, the energies of the world were fully engaged in what by 1915 was already known as the Great War. From the men in the trenches to the women and children on the home front, no one escaped the war. The suffering of soldiers and civilians was at the heart of the totalisation of the conflict; it was part of the combatant nations' great struggle for civilisation, from the actual war period through to the 1920s, 'from death to memory'.[1]

In essence, mental suffering was the same for civilians as for the mobilised men, and for many of them the war meant terrible deprivation; but it was the inhabitants of the invaded and then occupied regions – the people of northern and northeastern France, Belgium, Serbia, East Prussia and western Russia – who paid the highest price. Although historians justifiably reserve the epithet of 'total' for the Second World War and speak of aspects of totalisation in the first worldwide conflict, it is undoubtedly true that conditions in territory occupied between 1914 and 1918 turned it into a veritable 'laboratory', a first base from which to try and understand this century of political murder.

And yet this terrible warning was almost completely forgotten, and gave rise to a variety of myths. I would like to show here how

---

1. Annette Becker, *La guerre et la foi, de la mort à la mémoire*, Paris, Armand Colin, 1994. *War and Faith, the Religious Imagination in France, 1914-1930*, Oxford, Berg, 1998.

forgetting and mythification were constructed, and how the peoples of Europe, who would undergo far worse twenty years later, were unable to make use of past experience.

The Franco-Austrian sociologist Michael Pollack has brilliantly shown how the concentration-camp experience of the Second World War, precisely because it was so extreme, contained the potential for intellectual catharsis: 'Any extreme experience reveals the elements and conditions of "normal" experience, whose very familiarity often blocks analysis.'[2]

Using his methodological thinking as my starting point, I would like to show here that the various traumas suffered by the occupied people of northern France between 1914 and 1918 are an example of the complexity of the Great War – a complexity which is often forgotten, in a denial of memory by this section of the population, who were sorely tried, but whose war experience differed from that of the majority. It was probably the weight of their guilt, the sensation of belonging to a minority which must be subsumed into a majority experience – that of the nation at war – which engendered the drama of the ensuing years.

The Origins of Myth: The Trauma of Invasion and Occupation

From Reality to Myth: The Invasion

In the first weeks of the War, during the German advance, there were a number of incidents in which troops committed atrocities against civilians: villages burned, women raped, hostages shot. The Germans, who were genuinely obsessed with snipers (a memory of the 1870-71 war), suspected all civilians and were not inclined to show mercy. How could those who fled before the rapidly advancing troops not have circulated increasingly horrifying tales? The German armies did not respect the 1907 Hague Convention – surely therefore they must consist of criminals.

The War created and fostered violence and fear. Those who were advancing into enemy territory, the Germans, could only be barbarians. Their war was not, as was that of their adversaries, a just war. Furthermore, the destruction of churches and the execution of a number of priests proved that the Germans were in direct

2. Michael Pollack, 'Le témoignage' and 'La gestion de l'indicible', *Actes de la Recherche en Sciences Sociales*, Paris, June 1986, pp. 3-53.

confrontation with God. Tales proliferated of Belgians and French crucified by cheering old troopers; and of God's innocent children having their hands cut off. Many witnesses claimed to have met families in the exodus with children whose hands were wrapped in bandages.[3] Religious imagery was particularly powerful, and it is directly symptomatic of this time of fervent belief, when nation and the culture of war came together to form a 'war of religion'.[4] Surely God led the way in this struggle of each and every individual, in this war which had become a crusade?

From Myth to Reality: the Occupation

It is as part of this atmosphere, at once phantasmagorical and genuinely terrifying, characteristic of the early days of the war, that the occupation must be imagined. The local population, bewildered by the defeat, had to take in and feed in their own homes men whom they could see only as barbarians. In addition to their continually deteriorating living conditions, the civilians were forced to undergo experiences that they described as 'atrocities', frequently the result of the Germans' difficulty in obtaining their requisitioning demands.

Many situations which have become commonplace throughout the world in the last hundred years created constant distress and frequent incomprehension: hostage-taking, concentration camps,[5] forced labour, deportation, human shields, rape. Repression, resistance, clandestine press, individuals smuggled across frontiers, then fresh repression: the vicious circle of all wars against civilians.[6]

In northern France, hostage-taking began in the autumn of 1914, with local dignitaries, mayors, city councillors, industrialists, and in Lille even the bishop, being taken. Next came the deportation of younger men, taken to work as civil prisoners. The Great War saw many thresholds of violence overstepped, and as

3. A. Becker, *War and Faith*, Ch. 1; J. Horne 'Les mains coupées, "atrocités allemandes" et opinion française en 1914' in *Guerre et cultures, 1914-1918*, eds S. Audoin-Rouzeau, A.Becker, J.J.Becker, G.Krumeich, J.Winter, Paris, Armand Colin, 1994.

4. The expression comes from the writer Jacques Rivière, who was imprisoned in Germany during the war.

5. Used against civilians for the second time; the British had invented the system during the Boer War.

6. For a detailed study of the occupation, see my book *Oubliés de la Grande Guerre. Populations occupées, déportés civils, prisonniers de guerre. Humanitaire et culture de guerre*, Paris, Noêsis, 1998.

part of the process prisoners – civilian and military, transformed into pawns in the various stages of warfare – bore the full force of the drama as the conflict became universal, for example when one nation carried out reprisals against another. The worst feature was undoubtedly the use of prisoners as human shields, at the rear of the enemy lines, where they were hit by shells from their own armies. Forced to work for the enemy war effort, they bore a crushing sense of guilt: did not working for the enemy mean working against one's own nation?

While these dramatic events were unfolding, the inhabitants were terrified by the reality of the atrocities and the added blend of rumours. When women were seized and taken away in 1916, for example, there was a widespread rumour that 'they were being taken into the *Kommandantur* to have their breasts cut off'.[7] David Hirsch speaks of 'general stupidity' and, confronted with such lucidity, one must in turn quote Marc Bloch: 'A false news item always springs from the collective representations which predate it; it only *seems* to appear "by chance" ... it is impossible to overstate the extent to which emotion and weariness eliminate critical faculties.'[8]

But they certainly created a unique trauma. The continuing absence of any consensus in the French language on the meaning of the words 'trauma' and 'traumatism' is, I think, a revealing demonstration of this refusal to understand, both then and often still today.[9]

---

7. David Hirsch, war diary, 27 April 1916. Manuscript generously lent by his grandson, Jean-Pierre Hirsch, to whom I would like to express my thanks. See: *Journaux de combattants et de civils de la Grande Guerre* (ed. Annette Becker). Lille, Septentrion, 1998.

8. Marc Bloch, 'Réflexions d'un historien sur les fausses nouvelles de la guerre', *Revue de synthèse historique* XXXIII (1921):13-35.

9. The definitions in the *Dictionnaire Robert*, which represents authority in the world of language, strike me as sufficiently significant to be reproduced in full. (Latest edition, 1994, p. 2,299):

TRAUMA: n.m. (1876; Gr. *trauma*, 'wound'). Didact. Medical. Lesion or local wound produced by an external agent operating mechanically. Psych: (questioned use) Violent emotion which modifies the personality of a subject by sensitising it to emotions of similar type.

TRAUMATISM: n.m. (1855; Gr. *traumatismos*). 1. Med. Group of physical or psychological disturbances provoked in the organism by the trauma. Cranial traumatisms, multiple traumatisms (see polytraumatism). 2. Psych. and current. Psychical traumatism (or, erroneously, trauma): group of disturbances resulting from a violent emotional shock. – Psychoanalysis. Event setting off in a subject a flood of excitation exceeding the threshold of tolerance of its psychic capacity.

How to Overcome Trauma: Accuse the Enemy

> Optimism is the essential feature ... is it not the expression of our race, simultaneously confident and insubordinate, developing in intensity the more it suffered under the heavy German burden? A spirit that blends patriotism and plotting. ... The proliferation of hiding places to protect possessions from requisition. ... The inhabitants of the occupied lands generally exhibited magnificent morale in the face of the enemy, unflagging optimism, limitless confidence, the expression of the race's essential qualities.[10]

The term 'race' was used everywhere during the War, displaying a concept of the whole war as a struggle between two intrinsically opposed 'races'. Scientists and doctors in particular went very much further than the declarations of many intellectuals on both sides, that this was a war of civilisation. It was in biological terms that the contrast between French and Germans could/should be expressed. In their view, Germans who embarked on a war designed to 'weaken the French race' understood this. The doctors in the Nord (a department in northern France) who studied tuberculosis or famine-induced amenorrhoea among the occupied population agreed word for word with the conclusions of their colleagues studying the results of long imprisonment among prisoners held in Germany between 1914 and 1918. Germanophobia, eugenics and racism shared two complementary ideas: a positive concern, that 'the French race' should be preserved in its purity, and a negative concern, to prove the inferiority, perversion and perverting nature of 'the German race'.

Psychiatrists, on the other hand, sought to deny the increase in psychiatric cases during the War. Just as French doctors in general tended to treat men suffering from shock in the trenches as malingerers, bad Frenchmen trying to evade their military and patriotic duty, so the specialists from the Nord, convinced as they were of the unfailing patriotism of the inhabitants of their 'little nation', inevitably declined to record any pathology which might denote a refusal to support the War, which they only wanted to see as being bravely accepted. For them, total support for the War was taken for granted. Once shock sufferers were categorised as suffering from the burden of their heredity – preferably working-class and alcoholic – everything fell tidily into place.

10. Paul Assoignon, *Etat mental et Psychologie morbide en pays occupé, à Lille en particulier*, Medical dissertation, Lille, 21 July 1919, pp. 13, 81.

In their postwar struggle scientists thus matched the politicians of the Nord who sought recognition of the distinctive nature of the disasters of the war in their region, particularly to win reparations and war damages.

Even before the War ended, the socialists of the Nord had set the tone in the Chamber of Deputies. This tone of hatred is all the more significant because it came from socialists whom some might have suspected of peace-loving, or even pacifist, ideas.

> M. Delory: I have never favoured territorial conquest, I shall continue to oppose it. But not to claim a just peace would be a crime against France, a crime against humanity!

> M. Brunet: … *Monsieur le Président*, I demand publication of my colleague's speech, evidence of Germany's crimes against humanity.[11]

'Crime against humanity.' An expression with a full life ahead of it in the twentieth century. … All the more so, perhaps, because from the mid-1920s the trauma of the occupied North generally fell into oblivion. Because its victims were mainly women and, secondly, poor? Because the Nord did not wish to stand out as different, in a France reunited in peace? Because the militant pacifists demanded a battle for peace and not for a reminder of the atrocities of wartime, which could never match the supreme atrocity, war itself? Because the expression 'Post-traumatic stress syndrome' had not yet been invented and, in the French language of the late twentieth century, is only a translation of the English, just as 'shell shock' was translated during the war by *'obusite'* [from the French *obus*, shell]?

Forgetting and Denial: 1918-1942

No One Commemorates Trauma

In a war between nations, all forms of suffering are claimed by one camp or another; every life, every wound and every death is added to the tally. By 1915 France had organised the memory of the only people who counted as heroes, the dead soldiers. The heroism of the troops was enough for the bulk of people who passionately wanted to return to normality. Why should the living be commemorated when the only true heroes were the dead? Above all, why fight for a regional memory just when everyone believed

11. Session of 22 October 1918.

that victory came only from the nation's undivided effort? During the war the unanimity of the 'Sacred Union' had embraced all possible divisions, and now the unanimity of memory was similarly centred on one exclusive experience – the experience of the soldiers in the trenches – which tended towards a total disregard of any suffering that was anomalous or experienced by a minority.

The memory of the First World War held by civilians in the occupied region was comprehensively disregarded.[12] The War and its dead were remembered in the region because, as everywhere in France, the men went off to fight in August 1914. Commemorative monuments were constructed for these combatants of the north, just as everywhere else in France. A second level of memory stems from the geographical setting of these frontier regions, which was precisely one of the factors that made the occupation and the capture of civilian prisoners possible. But how should a war be commemorated when it had neither the name nor the glamour of a war? How should victims, as opposed to heroes, be commemorated? How to commemorate the incommemorable – hunger, cold, forced labour, rape, official or substitute hostages,[13] travel passes, requisitioning, fines, tuberculosis, and more…?

Why were these novel and serious forms of violence visited upon the inhabitants not dwelled upon? Initially, no doubt, material reparations took precedence, and the degree of destruction in the region also explains why the most substantial commemorative monuments were slow in being built.

In no time, the fact of having been excluded from the war of sacrifice by being too weak or too wretched, was bound to discredit mere witnesses – whether they were the victims, or the few humanitarian activists, who, by definition, could not take sides.

In the postwar period, the passions of war were substantially eclipsed by militant pacifism and its attempted denial of the overweening crusade element which had led to this worldwide disaster. The philosophy of ultimate pacifism replaced that of victory at any price, and the universal mood of the 1920s endorsed this conversion to the credo of peace which had been well prepared during the War itself. This attitude of consensus towards the mystique

---

12. Annette Becker, *Le Monde*, 6-7 November 1994: 'L'attachement du Nord à un passé combattant, résistant et pacifiste.' p. VIII. Ibid., 'D'une guerre à l'autre : mémoire de l'occupation et de la résistance: 1914-1940', *Revue du Nord*, no. 306 (July-September 1994):453-65.

13. The first mention of these categories is in the *Bulletin de Lille*, published under the control of the German authorities, no. 1, 15 November 1914.

of the War is probably the most difficult feature to explain today. Every nation committed itself beyond reason to this intense hope, the postwar feeling that war had been banished for ever in a new Golden Age.

From Myth to Propaganda, Approaching the Second World War

'Cyclical silences are not simply the result of prohibitions from on high; they may be the consequence of an interiorisation of feelings of inferiority, shame, or anticipated discrimination.'[14]

In 1921, it is true, Lille hosted a very large *'Exposition des Oeuvres Sociales'* (Exhibition of Social Work) designed to illustrate everything that was done for the inhabitants, hard-pressed by the war years and the demands of reconstruction. Social work (primarily concerned with families at that time), was relocated in a public health or even eugenicist context: the War was seen as a moment when these 'positive' concerns had been put at risk.

The exhibition organisers hoped that the incriminating documents would be preserved, and a museum of the invasion created 'in the chief town of each of our ten occupied departments. Then the great lessons of our distress and cruel treatment by a barbarian invader would be preserved for ever from oblivion and treacherous misrepresentation.'[15]

The project evidently never came to fruition, for the same reasons which led to the denial and then forgetting of the individual events in the lives of the occupied civilians. There was no question of recalling a period of distress which did not appear sufficiently heroic, any more than the efforts to provide help. The humanitarian challenges and those who had attempted to remedy them must be eliminated from memory.

Between 1914 and 1918 the peoples of Europe had discovered that war now meant more than conflict between the armies and the patriotic cultures of wholly mobilised nations. Beginning in 1931, Hitler linked his desire for a new order to deportation: 'Everywhere, people are awaiting a new world order. We intend to introduce a great resettlement policy. ... Think of the biblical deportations and the massacres of the Middle Ages... and remember the extermination of the Armenians.'[16]

14. Pollack, 'Le témoignage' et 'La gestion de l'indicible', p. 22.
15. *Nos familles sous le joug allemand*, leaflet published for the 1921 exhibition in the Palais Rameau, May 1921, Lille, p. 4.
16. Quoted by Vahakn Dadrian, *The History of the Armenian Genocide*, Oxford, Berghahn Books, 1995, p. 408.

And yet in 1939 the Führer was able to jeer at the failure of Europeans to remember the Armenian massacre of 1915: 'After all, who still speaks today of the elimination of the Armenians?'[17] Of all other aspects of the totalisation of war, beginning with the fate of the former occupied territories, even Hitler's cynicism retained no memory.

Beyond the confidence of assassins in their impunity, and their belief that the battle of death and memory had been settled once and for all, one wonders whether the pacifists' struggle, and the denial of specific recollections of the sufferings of the civilians in occupied territories, did not to some extent contribute to the obliteration of memory, and particularly the memory of some victims' sufferings.

In 1940 the writer Henri Calet was taken prisoner but escaped after seven months, and in 1942 described his experience of the rout two years earlier, in devastating fictional form. At the end of the book his hero-double gets back to Paris:

> I arrived at the Arc de Triomphe, I crossed the *Etoile*, distancing my mind somewhat from my true self, I stopped under the Arch, and there I said a quiet 'hallo' as I passed by, without any drums or trumpets, 'hallo' to that other chap, the one who was killed last time round. In my own name, and in the name of two million comrades. I understood better what he had undergone before he was buried. There were some flowers round his grave, no longer fresh but smelling foul. We were part of the same family, those who are assembled every twenty years on the battlefields for some strange harvest. ... Who or what did we suffer for, he and I? He who represented two million dead and I two million humiliated – without going further back in our history. For France. But why did she wish us so ill? Grey-clad soldiers stopped to salute him, impressively. Even there we were not alone.[18]

Here we can see, expressed with great literary skill, the culmination during the Second World War of the disgust felt by the veterans of the Great War at their crusading efforts for a cause which they could no longer decently defend. Between 1918 and the very beginning of the 1940s the veterans of the '*Der des Der*' (the 'war to end all wars'), combatants and civilians, created a screening process designed to damp down and obliterate their wartime ardour. These pessimistic attitudes have been studied more often

17. *Ibid.* p. 406.
18. Henri Calet, *Le Bouquet*, Paris, Gallimard, 1945, p. 292.

than the preceding fervour. Is it not always more exciting to trace cynicism and lost faith, than the beaming platitudes of those happy optimists possessed of simple faith?

The inescapable parallel is with the way in which the atrocities and acts of violence committed by various armies of invasion and occupation between 1914 and 1918 were forgotten or even denied. The reports drawn up from 1915 and 1916 onwards contained some irrefutable eyewitness accounts; they also included narratives which were recognised sooner or later as a form of myth, like those about hands being cut off. The Allied nations' propaganda, particularly from the British, and also the French and the Americans, faithfully circulated every crime, whether real or invented; so faithfully that from the war until the publication of the work of recent historians,[19] these 'atrocities' were often thought of as invention pure and simple. The baby was thrown out with the bathwater, on both sides of the political spectrum. Former combatants turned pacifist, especially the militant pacifists, thought of war itself as an atrocity, and it was therefore not necessary to put forward any account of exactions which might be neither more nor less than propaganda. This inevitably deflected the population from the true struggle to be undertaken, the fight against war itself. Atrocity propaganda therefore became the pacifists' scapegoat, the all-too-obvious explanation for the willingness of nations to fight each other, their consent to this tragedy which left ten million dead: they had been misled and it would not happen again.

Conclusion

In June 1940 Adolf Hitler came as a former soldier to see the trenches where he had fought twenty-five years earlier, and to see the military cemeteries. German blood had sanctified the soil of Flanders, and the new occupiers were encouraged to visit all the significant sites in the regions where their fathers had distinguished themselves.[20] On 22 June, Hitler insisted on signing the

---

19. In the forefront, John Horne and Allan Kramer, *German Atrocities 1914*, forthcoming, Cambridge University Press. Also: Stéphane Audoin-Rouzeau, *Le fils de l'Allemand*, Paris, Aubier, 1996; Annette Becker, 'Life in an occupied zone: Lille-Roubaix-Tourcoing, 1914-1918' in *Facing Armageddon. The First World War Experienced*, directed by Hugh Cecil and Peter Liddle, Leeds, 1995.

20. Etienne Dejonghe, 'Etre 'occupant' dans le Nord', *Revue du Nord* (octobre-decembre 1983):707-45.

armistice at Rethondes. The inscription marking the defeat of 1918 was hidden under a Nazi flag, but the Foch monument had been preserved – so that the stone General in Chief could witness the French disaster? In Hitler's eyes, Germany's humiliation at the end of the Great War was avenged, but the intense bitterness created by the defeat of 1918 – a bitterness which had turned to hatred, according to Hannah Arendt's analysis[21] – was henceforward to demonstrate its full capacity.

Just as, in 1914, the Germans' actions and reactions were often the result of the traumatising memories of the snipers of 1870, the inhabitants of the Nord saw the dramas of the occupation revived. This was the reason for the massive exodus. Every day during the campaign of May 1940, the newspapers of the Nord cited the example of the First World War. This time the atrocities took on a different dimension, as can be seen in the May massacres perpetrated by the S.S. Totenkopf (Death's Head) division at Aubigny-en-Artois, Courrières and Oignies.

Amongst the earliest Resistance activists of 1940, the initial decisions and the first ventures were based on memories of the Great War: information, escape networks, clandestine press. The graves of British soldiers were decorated with flowers as proof of goodwill towards Great Britain. In rural Pas-de-Calais it was often the older men, soldiers in the Great War, who formed the earliest networks for escape to England.[22]

This concept, of the manipulation of opinion based on the false reports of atrocities in 1914-18, can be found at the heart of the drama which was to become the very essence of the Second World War and of the whole century: that of the Holocaust. How could the extermination of the Jews in Europe be even hinted at to those who believed that the worst tales of the Great War had all been lies? In 1942 the Jewish publisher Victor Gollancz published a book in England, *Let My People Go*, to warn the British public of

21. Hatred, certainly not lacking in the pre-war world, began to play a central role in public affairs everywhere. ... Nothing perhaps illustrates the general disintegration of political life better than this vague, pervasive hatred of everybody and everything, without a focus for its passionate attention, with nobody to make responsible for the state of affairs. ... It consequently turned in all directions, haphazardly and unpredictably. ... This atmosphere of disintegration, though characteristic of the whole of Europe between the two wars, was more visible in the defeated than in the victorious countries.

Hannah Arendt, *The Origins of Totalitarianism*, 1951; London, George Allen and Unwin, 1967, p. 268.

22. See the article by René Lesage, 'Quelques aspects de la Résistance en Artois occidental', *Revue du Nord* LXXII (1990):1053-65.

what was happening in Poland. It opens with two pages in which he has to distinguish between what was *truly* happening in 1942 and the 'invention of atrocities' in the past.[23] In the same year, the Polish Jew Calel Perechodnik wrote his devastating account of the deportation of his family to Treblinka: 'Did you escape from Treblinka to tell the world lies about the might of Germany? Are you going to promote *Greuelpropaganda* (atrocity propaganda)?'[24]

What is particularly striking in this account is the general absence of the Germans. They are the promoters of a fiendish drama in which the actors are principally Polish, particularly Catholics, and Jews, including himself, since, as a member of the Jewish ghetto police, the author had been forced to shut his wife, his little girl, and his friends, into the cattle-trucks departing for the death camps.

What is striking, initially as a secondary consideration and then like a missing link which suddenly falls into its proper place on its own, is that a victim of the Holocaust is himself sending us back to the Great War, and in particular to one of its most mythified, distorted, forgotten and denied aspects, the 'German atrocities'. In 1942, it was too late to invent myths about atrocities.

Translated by Helen McPhail

23. I am grateful to John Horne for pointing out this reference.

24. Calel Perechodnik, *Suis-je un meurtrier?* Paris, Liana Levi, 1995, p. 86. Published in Poland in 1993. Original 1943 manuscript preserved at Yad Vashem, Jerusalem.

2

THE *MARSEILLAISE* AS MYTH AND METAPHOR

The Transfer of Rouget de Lisle to The Invalides during the Great War

Avner Ben-Amos

The gradual coming to power of the republicans in the French Third Republic during the late 1870s meant that, as François Furet put it, 'The French Revolution entered the harbour.'[1] The collapse of the Old Regime pushed the French state into turbulent political waters: between 1789 and 1879 the country was governed by several types of political regimes, most of which were hostile to the Revolution. The establishment of the long-lasting Third Republic did not put an end to the controversies surrounding the meaning and legacy of the Revolution, but that momentous event gained an important place in the outlook of the new regime.[2] It was claimed to be the sacred origin of the regime, and its ideals were said to be those of the young Republic. A series of symbolic gestures underlined the connection between the Revolution and the republican regime: the *Marseillaise* became the national anthem in 1879, and the anniversary of the storming of the Bastille (14 July) was declared a national holiday in the following year. The Revo-

1. François Furet, *La Révolution*, Vol. 2, *Terminer la Révolution (1814-1880)*, Paris, Hachette, 1988, p. 467.

2. For the image of the French Revolution during the Third Republic see Robert Gildea, *The Past in French History*, New Haven, Yale University Press, 1994, pp. 13-61.

lutionary cult of great men was resumed in 1885 when the Pantheon reopened its gates to the body of Victor Hugo on the occasion of the poet's national funeral. Four years later, the centenary of the French Revolution was officially celebrated through, among other symbolic acts, the transfer of the bodies of three Revolutionary generals and a republican deputy to the Pantheon. The Revolution had also a prominent role in the history lessons and civic education of the new republican schools that were established by the regime. It was the event around which the French past was organised, and which gave meaning to everything that preceded and followed it.[3]

The cult of the Revolution, which diminished in scope and intensity around the turn of the century, was rekindled after 1905, as a result of the nationalist revival that engulfed both the republican camp and the extreme Right.[4] The 1912 bicentennial of the birth of Rousseau was celebrated with great pomp, and the 14 July anniversary again became a major national holiday, an occasion to show enthusiasm for army and flag. No wonder, then, that when the Great War came, the Revolution was 'mobilised' to serve the propagandistic efforts of the regime.

The Revolutionary past had already been put to use unofficially on the eve of the war, during the funeral of Jean Jaurès. The socialist leader had been assassinated by a fanatic nationalist who wanted to stop the efforts to prevent the war, but the funeral turned into a workers' demonstration supporting the belligerent policy of the government.[5] One of the tricolour flags carried in the procession was inscribed with the word 'Valmy', referring to the first victory of the Revolutionary armies in 1792. The speech of the workers' union (Confédération Générale du Travail) leader, Léon Jouhaux, included a reference to the 'soldiers of the [Revolutionary] year II', and he portrayed the Germans as the enemies of democracy, much as the Prussians had been depicted during the Revolution.[6] The current situation was thus 'redescribed' in terms

---

3. See Mona Ozouf, 'La Révolution : l'école', in *L'Ecole de la France : Essais sur la Révolution, l'utopie et l'enseignement*, Paris, Gallimard, 1984, pp. 231-49.

4. Eugen Weber, *The Nationalist Revival in France 1905-1914*, Berkeley, University of California Press, 1968.

5. For Jaurès's funeral see Avner Ben-Amos, 'La panthéonisation de Jean Jaurès. Rituel et politique pendant la IIIe République', *Terrain* 15 (1990):49-64.

6. For Jouhaux's speech and its significance, see Annie Kriegel and Jean-Jacques Becker, *1914, La guerre et le mouvement ouvrier français*, Paris, Armand Colin, 1964, pp. 135-43.

of the confrontation between the French Revolutionaries and their enemies, a metaphorical shift that often recurred during the war. Metaphor, argue Lakoff and Johnson, is not 'only' a linguistic phenomenon; its basis is cognitive, and it helps us structure our perception of the world by means of explaining one thing in terms of another.[7] The new and threatening reality of the Great War could thus be rendered more intelligible when apprehended in terms of the successful wars of the French Revolution. No one, of course, believed that they were actually revisiting the experience of the Revolutionary wars. As Frye remarks, about the nature of metaphor, 'there is, or seems to be, an assertion that A is B, along with an undercurrent of significance that tells us that A is obviously not B.'[8] This tension between the 'is' and the 'as-if' does not diminish the power of a metaphor, but is of its very essence and increases its effectiveness. Analysing the cognitive aspects of metaphorical thinking, Apter notes an effect of synergy, which is produced 'by the conjunction of mutually exclusive meanings'. He describes this effect as 'increased vividness associated with enhanced arousal.'[9]

The ways to evoke the memory of the Revolutionary wars were many, but one of the most popular and efficient methods was to organise a communal singing of the *Marseillaise* or refer to it in other media. The national anthem usually symbolised the nation as a whole, but within the proper staging it also carried a more specific, historical connotation. Making the *War Song for the Army of the Rhine* – the original name of the anthem – stand for the entire French military effort of the 1790s was the equivalent of using another literary trope: metonymy. Lodge, following Roman Jakobson, makes a sharp distinction between metaphor, in which one thing substitutes for another, and metonymy, in which a part or an attribute refers to a whole through a relation of contiguity.[10] Accordingly, these tropes belong to two different linguistic and

7. George Lakoff and Mark Johnson, *Metaphors We Live By*, Chicago, University of Chicago Press, 1980, pp. 3-6.

8. Northrop Frye, 'The Koine of Myth : Myth as a Universally Intelligible Language', in *Myth and Metaphor, Selected Essays, 1974-1988*, Charlottesville, University of Virginia Press, 1991, p. 7.

9. Michael J. Apter, 'Metaphor as Synergy', in David S. Miall (ed.), *Metaphor : Problems and Perspectives*, Brighton, The Harvester Press, 1982, p. 56.

10. Since metonymy and synecdoche are closely related, I will use here only the former term. See David Lodge, *The Modes of Modern Writing: Metaphor, Metonymy, and the Typology of Modern Literature*, Ithaca, Cornell University Press, 1977, pp. 73-124.

cognitive axes: the metaphoric axis of selection, based on similarity and substitution, and the metonymic axis of combination, based on conjoining several entities to create a message.[11] Applied to the present case, it follows that the decision to choose the Revolutionary wars among the Franco-German wars as a lens through which to look at the Great War belongs to the metaphorical axis of selection. In contrast, using the *Marseillaise* together with other symbolic elements to evoke the memory of the Revolutionary wars belongs to the axis of combination. The effort to generate enthusiasm around the wars of the French Revolution peaked early in the war, on 14 July 1915, when the body of Rouget de Lisle, the writer of the *Marseillaise*, was solemnly transferred to the Invalides. This event can be regarded as what Barthes named a syntagm, i.e., a certain combination of signs that, like a sentence, conveys a particular meaning.[12] Each of the components of the event – the time, the place and the person who was honoured by the act – constituted, separately, a metonymy that stood for the French Revolution, and together they constituted a complete statement concerning the heroism of the Revolutionary armies.

The aim of the present article is to analyse de Lisle's reinterment as an example of the metaphorical uses of the French Revolutionary wars for propagandistic purposes during the Great War. The analysis is based on the assumption that in both metaphor and metonymy the act of comparison highlights certain aspects of the compared entities while effacing others. The complexity of the French Revolution and the multiple meanings of the *Marseillaise* were thus reduced during the war to enlist them in the service of propaganda and to boost public morale. However, this reductive usage had a long tradition of its own, going back to the time of the French Revolution. I will proceed, therefore, by briefly tracing the variegated history of the main symbolic elements that appeared in the transfer of Rouget de Lisle to the Invalides, and then by analysing the event itself as a unique syntagm that was the result of a particular reading of these elements.

Any investigation of the metaphorical uses of the French Revolution should not ignore the fact that at the beginning of the twen-

---

11. The distinction between these two axes is analogous to that between *langue*/paradigm/system/code and *parole*/syntagm/message. See Lodge, *The Modes of Modern Writing…*, p. 74.

12. Roland Barthes, *Elements of Semiology*, trans. Annette Lavers and Colin Smith, New York, Hill and Wang, 1968, pp. 58-88.

tieth century the Revolution was also considered an important – for some the most important – segment of the French past. Such segments are usually represented through narrative forms, which give the disparate events a coherent structure and particular meaning. Narratives, as Bruce Lincoln claims in *Discourse and the Construction of Society*, can be classified not by their content but by the claims that are made on their behalf by their narrators. Using this classification one can distinguish between myth, which sets up a model for society, and history, which does not.[13] The French Revolution functioned as such a myth during the Great War, when it acquired special significance as an exemplary event. Likewise, one could argue that through the constant narration of the circumstances of its composition by Rouget de Lisle and its usage during the Revolutionary wars, the *Marseillaise* was more than a song: it had become a myth.

The transfer of de Lisle to the Invalides[14] was, then, an opportunity to retell the myths associated with the *Marseillaise* and make them palpable. The affinity between myth and ritual has already been noted by anthropologists and literary critics, who have pointed out that they can be different modes of communicating the same message.[15] Ritual is thus capable of using duration and various theatrical means to recount the story that is told by the written myth. According to Frye, myth has the power to annihilate the time that separates past and present, and the same is also true for ritual.[16] Time in ritual is of a special kind, since it is framed in a way that sets it apart from everyday life, and when it commemorates a certain extraordinary event past and present become one. This is especially true in anniversaries of birth and beginning, which imply a return to the original, commemorated event.[17] Through an antithetical mechanism that resembles that of metaphor, such rituals both declare that the event in the present recreates the event in the past,

---

13. Bruce Lincoln, *Discourse and the Construction of Society: Comparative Studies of Myth, Ritual, and Classification*, New York, Oxford University Press, 1989, pp. 23-26.

14. The initial plan was to transfer the body of Rouget de Lisle to the Pantheon, but because of last-minute legal complications it was decided to transfer it to the Invalides.

15. Edmund Leach, *The Political System of Highland Burma*, London, Bell, 1954, pp. 13-14. See also Walter Burkert, *Structure and History in Greek Mythology and Ritual*, Berkeley, University of California Press, 1979; Frye, 'The Koine of Myth', pp. 6-7; Lincoln, *Discourse*, pp. 5-7.

16. Frye, 'The Koine of Myth', p. 7.

17. See Mircea Eliade, *Cosmos and History: The Myth of the Eternal Return*, New York, Garland, 1985.

and assert that this recreation is impossible. The ritual of 14 July 1915 marked a dual birth – of the *Marseillaise*, and the French Revolution – and indicated a return to that sacred time, but it also underlined the current situation of the war.

But before returning to the wars of French Revolution, of which the *Marseillaise* functioned as a metonymy, it is necessary to explain their selection from among the other Franco-German conflicts that could also have served as points of reference. The answer seems to lie in the unique characteristics of the Revolutionary wars, which made them exemplary: they were the only episode in the French past in which a republican regime, like the one that was governing during the Great War, triumphed over a German power. In the other encounters Frenchmen were either led to victory by monarchical figures (Louis XIV and Napoleon Bonaparte) or were defeated by the Germans (the 1870-71 war). The Republic preferred, then, to evoke the episode with which it could identify, and which ended in victory.

All the symbolic elements that appeared in the transfer of de Lisle were related to the French Revolution. Even though some of them originated in the period before 1789, the Revolution marked them in a way that radically changed their meaning. My point of departure is, therefore, the era of the Revolution, and the transformations until the Great War in the meaning of each element will be separately delineated.

The Songwriter

Joseph Rouget de Lisle was neither a poet, nor a professional composer. He wrote the lyrics and the music of the *Marseillaise* in April 1792 while stationed in the garrison of Strasbourg, on the French eastern border, serving in the Revolutionary army as a military engineer. De Lisle had been born thirty-two years earlier, in a family of local dignitaries, and was allowed to add to his name the aristocratic particle that enabled him to attend military school.[18] He served as an officer in several garrison towns between 1784-89, while developing at the same time his talents as an amateur musician and lyricist. The outbreak of the Revolution attracted him to

18. See the biographical sketch of de Lisle in Michel Vovelle, 'La *Marseillaise*: La guerre ou la paix', in Pierre Nora, ed., *Les Lieux de mémoire*, 7 vols, Paris, 1984-92, Gallimard, Vol. 1, *La République*, 1984, pp. 85-136.

Paris, where he tried to make himself a name as an artist, with only modest success. He rejoined the army in 1791 and became part of the patriotic and Revolutionary salon of Dietrich, the mayor of Strasbourg, during a period of intense popular mobilisation against the foreign enemies. After the Revolutionary declaration of war against Austria on 20 April 1792 the mayor, dissatisfied with the current repertoire of patriotic and Revolutionary songs, asked de Lisle to write a new one, to fit the special circumstances. The result was the *War Song for the Army of the Rhine*, written overnight and first sung by Dietrich himself in his salon six days after the war had been declared. The song became quickly known in other parts of France, turning into one of the most popular Revolutionary hymns, and under the name of the *Marseillaise* had a long and complicated life of its own, which will be described separately in this chapter.

De Lisle remained for a while in the Revolutionary army, but had to leave in 1793 because of his misgivings about the radical phase of the Revolution, which began in August 1792 with the arrest of the king. He returned to Paris, spent a brief period in prison, but was 'rehabilitated' by the Thermidorians[19] and even given a special award of two violins by the Convention in gratitude for services rendered to the Revolution. He continued to write lyrics and to compose, for example, a *Hymn to Reason* and an anti-Robespierre song, but the *Marseillaise* remained his only lasting achievement. His Revolutionary outlook can be summarised as moderate: neither a monarchist, nor a Jacobin, he supported a liberal, republican regime and remained consistent in his faith until his death.

The post-Revolutionary fate of de Lisle bore out this consistency. Napoleon Bonaparte regarded him with suspicion because of his republican tendencies, and kept him under surveillance. During the Bourbon restoration, which was even more hostile to the Revolution, his situation worsened as his works were barred from the stage and he could barely earn his living. Only the 1830 Revolution and the advent of Louis-Philippe of Orléans to the throne changed his luck. The new Citizen-King drew part of his legitimacy from the moderate phase of the French Revolution, and he provided the author of the *Marseillaise* with a modest annual pension until his death in 1836, at the age of seventy-six. De Lisle was buried in Choisy-le-Roi, a small town near Paris, where he

---

19. Thermidor, Year II of the French Revolution: the turbulent period in July 1794 which led to the fall of Robespierre.

had spent the last years of his life as a half-forgotten artist, identi-fied mainly with his Revolutionary hymn.

The first attempt to transfer the image of de Lisle to the realm of myth was made in his lifetime by the republican sculptor David d'Angers, who created a large marble medallion bearing his por-trait in 1829.[20] It was sold for the benefit of the impoverished de Lisle in 1830, and its reproduction was included in most of his biographies and on numerous scores of the *Marseillaise*. The biographies began to appear in the early 1840s, and many of those that were published in the nineteenth century had the structure of a legendary tale, in which the life of the hero was centred around a single, exceptional deed – in de Lisle's case, the writing of the *Marseillaise*. Another means of commemoration – the statue – was also enlisted on his behalf,[21] but success was far from immediate. The first project of a public statue, initiated in 1838 by the muni-cipality of his native city, Lons-le-Saunier, was blocked by the gov-ernment of Louis-Philippe which had become more authoritarian and regarded homage to a Revolutionary figure with suspicion. The erection of the statue had to wait for the advent of the repub-licans to power in the Third Republic, and it was inaugurated in 1882, the same year in which another statue of de Lisle was inau-gurated in Choisy-le-Roi.

However, the most enduring image of de Lisle was associated with the 1848 Revolution. The triumph of the Republic made the author of the *Marseillaise* popular, and the painter Isidore Pils pre-sented in the salon of 1849 a painting named 'Rouget de Lisle singing the *Marseillaise* for the first time at the house of Dietrick (*sic*), Mayor of Strasbourg' (Figure 1). Even though the first public rendering of the song had been given, as we have seen, by the mayor himself,[22] the author – a young, handsome officer – was more appropriate for the role. De Lisle is shown standing in the middle of the salon, his dark figure contrasting with a white screen behind him, singing enthusiastically, in a theatrical pose, while a small audience looks at him with great attention. The painting was bought by the State, but was deposited at the Min-

20. For the various manifestations of the cult of de Lisle, see Christian Amalvi and Chantal Georgel, *Une Icône républicaine : Rouget de Lisle chantant La Marseillaise par Isidore Pils, 1849*, Paris, La Réunion des Musées Nationaux, 1989.

21. See Maurice Agulhon, 'La "statuomanie" et l'histoire', *Ethnologie française* 8, no. 2-3 (1978):145-72.

22. Vovelle, '*La Marseillaise*', p. 89.

Figure 1 *Isidore Pils, 'Rouget de Lisle singing the Marseillaise for the first time in the house of Dietrick (sic), Mayor of Strasbourg'. Reproduced by permission of the Musée Historique de Strasbourg.*

istry of the Interior; the public could see it again only in 1879, after the triumph of the republicans, when it was transferred to the Luxembourg museum. It had an immediate and immense success: it drew a large crowd of spectators daily and an exceptional number of copyists, who were encouraged by the growing demand of the State and numerous municipalities for copies of the celebrated painting. Reproductions appeared in republican history and civic education textbooks, where it served as an icon of Revolutionary élan. The nationalist revival that preceded the Great War made it even more popular, and during the war it was often used for propaganda, usually in conjunction with the *Marseillaise* (Figure 2).

Rouget de Lisle was both Revolutionary and patriot. During the French Revolution one could not easily distinguish between these two facets, for defending the Revolution meant also defending *la patrie* against the foreign enemies. Moreover, this fatherland was defined in republican terms, as a place where all the citizens were sovereign, hence their willingness to fight for it. However, as French history of the nineteenth and twentieth centuries has demonstrated, being a patriot does not always mean that one is

Figure 2 *Jean Carlu, 'La Marseillaise', November 1918. Collection du Musée d'Histoire Contemporaine – Bibliothèque de Documentation Internationale Contemporaine (BDIC). Copyright © Adagp, Paris, 1999.*

also a Revolutionary, or vice versa. For example, the extreme-right movement *Action française* that appeared around the turn of the century was patriotic but monarchist. The various symbolic elements that made up the transfer of de Lisle to the Invalides were both patriotic and Revolutionary, yet throughout their post-Revolutionary history only one of these facets was dominant at a time. The transfer itself was, above all, a patriotic act, though the Revolution was not totally absent from the event.

The Song

The *Marseillaise*, as we have seen, was born under the dual sign of imminent war and continuous revolution, and its words are a testimony to this duality. It opens with an exhortation to *'les enfants de la patrie'* (children of the fatherland) to go, arm themselves, form battalions and fight the enemy who is about to invade the country. The enemy has specific characteristics: it is composed of kings, tyrants and despots, who want to turn the Frenchmen into slaves. They will fight the representatives of the Old Regime in the name of *'l'amour sacré de la patrie'* (sacred love for the fatherland) – the fatherland being, in this case, both France and the Republic. Though the *Marseillaise* was a war song, it was sung by soldiers who fought for a revolution, and was identified therefore with the Republic. Vovelle distinguishes between a warlike *Marseillaise* of the frontiers and a Revolutionary one of the town squares,[23] but during the Revolution the movement of the song between the square and the frontier was rather smooth. The most celebrated example was that of the radical, volunteer soldiers of Marseilles, who arrived in Paris in summer 1792 on their way to the northern frontier, diffusing the song all along their route, thus giving it its name.

The *Marseillaise* was sung at many important Revolutionary and military events, such as the storming of the palace of Tuileries on 10 August 1792, and the victories of the battles of Valmy (20 September 1792) and Jemappes (6 November 1792). Its popularity received official recognition when the Convention decided at first that it would replace the Christian *Te Deum* (29 September 1792), and subsequently made it the national anthem (14 July 1795). In addition to its appearance in numerous theatrical and operatic performances, it was incorporated into the civic festivals of the Republic, and 'exported' with the Revolutionary armies to the conquered countries. The *Marseillaise*, due to its dual nature, succeeded in crossing the turbulent period of the Revolution intact, but the coming to power of Napoleon Bonaparte put an end to its official status.

During most of the nineteenth century, when France was governed by a series of monarchist and authoritarian regimes, hostile to the ideals of the French Revolution, the hymn was considered subversive because of its Revolutionary connotations. Its performance was either completely banned, or barely tolerated, while the republican opposition used it to mobilise and encourage its members in street demonstrations, prison gatherings, and other forms of collective action. In the revolutions of 1830 and 1848, and again during the 1871 Parisian Commune, it briefly emerged from clandestinity and was heard on barricades and in festivals that celebrated the victories of the opposition, but after the 'taming' of the revolutions it soon returned to its previous status. However, there were also certain historical moments when the hymn was recruited for patriotic purposes by monarchist regimes, as in the 'oriental' crisis of winter 1840, and after the declaration of war on Prussia in summer 1870.

---

23. Ibid., p. 96.

After becoming the official anthem of the Third Republic, the *Marseillaise* gradually became associated less with revolution than with patriotism. The conservative republicans who held power claimed to represent the ideals of the French Revolution, but they opposed any contemporary revolutionary act, arguing for slow social and economic reforms. At the same time they attempted to unify the country around a patriotic common denominator, never forgetting the humiliating defeat to Prussia and the lost territories of the east. The *Marseillaise* was thus used for pedagogical purposes in republican schools and civic festivals, becoming familiar to every citizen in its shortened and militaristic version. Meanwhile it was replaced among the workers by the *Internationale*, which was composed in 1888, and was considered a better expression of their revolutionary aspirations, notably after the turn of the century.[24] On the eve of the Great War the *Marseillaise* had almost entirely shed its revolutionary connotations, but as an official song, used only on solemn occasions, it generated little enthusiasm. The war did not change its meaning, but gave it a new life.

The Time

The violent storming of the Bastille, the fortress that was the symbol of the arbitrary power of the king, was immediately conceived by contemporaries as an epoch-making event. As Charles Péguy noted, it was 'actually a festival, the first celebration, the first commemoration and, so to speak, the first anniversary of the storming of the Bastille. Or, finally, its zeroth anniversary.'[25] However, the meaning of the event, which is commemorated in France annually, either by the authorities or by the opposition, has known several changes. The same patriotic/Revolutionary duality that characterised the *Marseillaise* was also typical of the celebration of 14 July 1789, but the relationship between the two aspects was somewhat different.[26]

24. See Marc Ferro, *L'Internationale : Histoire d'un chant de Pottier et Degeyter*, Paris, Noêsis, 1996.

25. Charles Péguy, *Clio*, Paris, Gallimard, 1932, pp. 114-15.

26. For the celebration of 14 July, see Jean-Pierre Bois, *Histoire des 14 Juillet 1789-1914*, Rennes, Editions Ouest-France, 1991; Rosemonde Sanson, *Les 14 juillet, fête et conscience nationale 1789-1975*, Paris, Flammarion, 1976; Christian Amalvi, 'Le 14 Juillet, du *Dies irae* à Jour de fête', in Nora, ed., *Les Lieux de mémoire*, Vol. I, pp. 421-72.

The first anniversary of the event was celebrated in Paris as the Festival of Federation, a commemoration that was meant to mark the unity of the nation both as a unified space and a harmonious, egalitarian society. The desire to unify the nation was part and parcel of the Revolutionary outlook, and during the following years the annual celebration retained this original meaning. Yet as the young Republic became more engaged in warfare, so did the celebration of Bastille Day become more militaristic and patriotic. Reference to the foreign threat was a good way to underline the need for unity, hence the presence of the army in Parisian and provincial ceremonies, serving as a patriotic sign. Very often the same 14 July ceremony included both a symbolic re-enactment of the storming of the Bastille and a military parade, thus representing both the Revolutionary and the patriotic aspects.

The coming to power of Napoleon Bonaparte signalled the end of the official celebration of Bastille Day, which was considered too subversive by the authoritarian Emperor. All the other, reactionary, regimes of nineteenth-century France also prohibited the observance of the anniversary, and even the Second Republic, which evolved from the 1848 revolution, hesitated to celebrate a date associated with revolutionary violence. Meanwhile, during most of the nineteenth century, the republican opposition tried to keep it clandestinely, marking the day with private banquets and gatherings, thus accentuating its revolutionary connotation.

After the fall of the Second Empire in 1870, the republicans began a nationwide campaign for the restitution of the celebration of 14 July, but they had to wait until 1880 for it to become officially the national holiday. The decree aroused fierce parliamentary debate between the republicans and the Royalist opponents of the celebration, who regarded the occasion as an instance of criminal bloodshed, not worthy of commemoration. As a compromise, it was decided that the new national holiday would be an anniversary of both the storming of the Bastille and the Festival of Federation.

The first celebration of the anniversary, in 1880, also became a model for the later celebrations of the Third Republic. Like the 1790 Festival of Federation, it was to be a display of national unity rather than an evocation of the violent conflict between Revolutionaries and their adversaries. The main official event was a military ceremony at the Parisian hippodrome of Longchamps, in which the President of the Republic, Jules Grévy, distributed flags to reconstituted army units that paraded afterwards in front of an enormous enthusiastic crowd. The rest of the day was dedicated to popular festivities in the decorated streets and squares of the capital, including dancing, drinking, and various games. These two elements, the military-patriotic, represented by a military parade, and the unitary-popular, continued to be the main poles of the celebration, while the Revolutionary aspect remained neglected. The popularity of the anniversary fluctuated from year to year, and the Royalist and Catholic Right persisted in its opposition, but 14 July remained the most important civic festival of the Republic until the outbreak of the Great War.

The Place(s)

Any analysis of the place of the ceremony should begin by a distinction between the intended and the actual place. The government's original plan was to transfer de Lisle to the Pantheon, an act that necessitated special legislation. However, since it was a last-moment decision, taken when both Houses were already in recess for the summer, it was decided to transfer the body to the Invalides, an act for which a decree was enough.[27] The Pantheon was the first choice of the republican government, yet when one looks forward to the postwar period, it is evident that the eventual choice of the Invalides anticipated subsequent developments in the commemorative policy of the regime. The transfer of de Lisle, therefore, came to constitute a turning point as the result of a coincidence, and could be perceived as such only with hindsight. The meaning of both the Pantheon and the Invalides, as two republican monuments that complemented each other, had first been established during the French Revolution, and it is to this that one should turn in order to understand later developments.

On the eve of the Revolution, the Pantheon was an almost-finished church, built in sumptuous, neoclassical style, and dedicated to Saint Geneviève, the patron saint of Paris who had saved the capital from the army of Attila the Hun.[28] The Revolutionaries, who were looking for a suitable monument to celebrate their 'great men' – scientists, philosophers, legislators – desacralised it, renamed it

27. The government decision to transfer the body of de Lisle to the Pantheon was formally taken on 10 July 1915, and the Invalides was chosen as a substitute on 13 July 1915. See Raymond Poincaré, *Au Service de la France. Neuf Années de Souvenirs*, 11 vols, Paris, Plon, 1930, Vol. 6, pp. 317-20.

28. For the history of the Pantheon since its inception, see *Le Panthéon, Symbole des Révolutions*, (Centre canadien d'architecture), Paris, Picard, 1989.

after the Roman temple, and turned it into a burial site. The first person to be buried there was the Revolutionary tribune, Mirabeau, who had died in April 1791, and he was followed by Voltaire (July 1791), the Revolutionary martyrs Lepeletier and Marat (January and July 1793, respectively), and Rousseau (October 1794). Although the bodies of Lepeletier and Marat were removed from the Pantheon as a result of the Thermidorian reaction, the monument continued to represent the civic ideals of the Revolution and to serve as the focal point of civic festivals until Napoleon's rise to power.

Like the Pantheon, the Invalides was also a creation of the Old Regime that was transformed by the Revolution, but it represented the latter's military and patriotic aspects.[29] It was built by Louis XIV as a military hospital and a place of retirement for old soldiers, and included a church and a royal chapel. In 1792 it was 'nationalised' and desacralised, but it continued to have the same functions, while playing a minor role in the cult of the Revolution. Under Napoleon, who owed his career to his military success, its symbolic importance increased: it hosted the ceremonies marking the victory of the battle of Marengo (1800) and the creation of the Order of the Legion of Honour (1804), and became a necropolis for the military heroes of France. The first body to be transferred there was that of Henri Turenne, the famous seventeenth-century commander (1800), soon followed by the bodies of Napoleon's military commanders who fell in his various European campaigns. In addition, the Invalides continued to fulfil its previous functions, while its church and chapel were resacralised, thus confirming the traditional ties between the army and the Church.

During the nineteenth century, the Invalides continued to receive the bodies of high-ranking army officers, but it was increasingly identified with the cult of Napoleon. The body of the Emperor, who had died on Saint Helena, was buried there in a magnificent ceremony (December 1840), and Napoleon III erected an impressive tomb for his uncle (1861), around which were buried other members of the Bonaparte family. The republicans of the Third Republic, who opposed Bonapartism as a form of dangerous dictatorship, did not change the status of this military institution, but diminished its symbolic role. They preferred, instead, to desacralise the Pantheon, which had been given back to the Church by Napoleon, and use it as a republican temple for the

---

29. For the history of the Invalides, see *Les Invalides : Trois siècles d'histoire*, Paris, Musée de l'Armée, 1974.

'great men' of the regime. After the centenary of the French Revolution, the Pantheon received the bodies of Sadi Carnot, the assassinated President of the Republic (1894), the scientist Marcelin Berthelot and his wife (1907), and the writer Emile Zola (1908). Transferring the body of de Lisle to the monument that was identified with the French Revolution, and which had already been the burial site of three Revolutionary generals would have been, therefore, only 'natural'. Using the Invalides, instead, for the same purpose meant that the military-patriotic aspect of the event was accentuated, notwithstanding the irony resulting from burying de Lisle in a monument dominated by the person who had restricted his freedom, suspecting him of political treason.

The Ritual of 14 July 1915

The ceremony in which the body of de Lisle was transferred to the Invalides was, in fact, a second burial. While a funeral is a rite of passage that includes elements of commemoration, in a second burial the commemorative aspect becomes dominant, especially if the event occurs many years after the death, and there is no one left to personally mourn the deceased.[30] However, even in such a commemorative ceremony the body – or, rather, the coffin – of the dead hero is needed, since it serves as the focal point of the event, and constitutes a palpable object with which the spectators can identify. The transfers to the Pantheon which took place in 1889 and 1908 were second burials, hence commemorations, but their aims were also related to the current political situation: the first ceremony commemorated the French Revolution, but it also meant to demonstrate that the Republic was no less patriotic than the popular general Boulanger, who was threatening the regime; the second ceremony commemorated the life and work of Zola, who had died in 1902, but it also the marked the final acquittal of Alfred Dreyfus, whose case had been vigorously defended by the novelist. Likewise, the transfer of de Lisle to the Invalides commemorated the Revolutionary captain who had written the national anthem, but was also related to the situation of the country at the end of the first year of the war, as we shall presently see.

30. In tribal societies, a second burial serves, at times, as a second rite of passage. See Robert Hertz, 'Contribution : une étude sur la représentation collective de la mort', in *Sociologie Religieuse et Folklore*, Paris, Presses Universitaires de France, 1970, pp. 1-83.

At the beginning of the summer of 1915, illusions of a quick and painless victory had already faded. After the early German success the front line stabilised, and a series of French attacks in winter and spring 1915 failed to change the situation. The army losses were great and its morale deteriorated as the horrible war of the trenches became a daily reality. The Sacred Union government of René Viviani, which represented all the political parties, knew that civilian morale was important, since without the support of the 'home front' combatants might not hold out. It made, therefore, a great effort to analyse the nation's morale systematically and to control it through press and other forms of censorship. But despite the difficulties and the disillusionment, Frenchmen were still relatively optimistic, convinced of their country's righteousness and confident that victory would come in a few months' time;[31] the breakdown of the Sacred Union came only much later, in spring 1917.

Under these circumstances it was clear that the first wartime 14 July could not be an ordinary celebration. With the soldiers fighting and dying at the front, and the civilian population suffering hardship as a result of the war economy, the previous, joyous manner of commemorating the French Revolution was inappropriate. On the other hand, the war only made a celebration, which underlined the unity of the nation and its glorious past, even more necessary. Hence the circular of Jean-Louis Malvy, the Minister of the Interior, prohibiting 'any activity that has the character of public rejoicing: banquets, parties, illuminations, fireworks, etc.,' while stressing the need for a dignified celebration, that would be 'exclusively patriotic and commemorative.'[32]

That the *Marseillaise* would feature as the main theme of the occasion was almost self-evident. The outbreak of war had made the national anthem popular again; it was sung in theatres, *cafés-concerts*, and in the streets as it expressed, and undoubtedly helped to create, the patriotic fervour of the mobilisation.[33] As the journal *L'Illustration* observed, 'This sublime song, which mobilised the volunteers of 1792 against the invader, is still today the one that rouses the national spirit.'[34] But the *Marseillaise*, as a song, was too

31. See Jean-Jacques Becker, *The Great War and the French People*, trans. Arnold Pomerans, Leamington Spa, Berg, 1985.
32. Quoted in Sanson, *Les 14 juillet*, p. 107.
33. For a subtle analysis of the French reaction to the mobilisation, see Jean-Jacques Becker, *1914, Comment les Français sont entrés dans la Guerre*, Paris, Presses de la Fondation Nationale des Sciences Politiques, 1977.
34. Quoted in Bois, *Histoire des 14 Juillet*, p. 243.

abstract and could not by itself form the centre of a ritual. Its writer, in contrast, was the perfect metonymy for both the hymn and the Revolutionary army: his figure evoked the heroic narrative of the fight against the foreign enemy, and the transfer of his body was part of the well-established ceremonial tradition of the Third Republic, thus creating an impression of continuity and stability, so much needed in the uncertain period of war.

The structure of the ceremony was that of a typical rite of passage: a phase of separation in Choisy-le-Roi, during which de Lisle was taken out from among the other, 'common' dead; a phase of transition, that included a procession through the streets of Paris, from the Arc de Triomphe, along the Champs Elysées and across the Alexandre III bridge, to the Invalides; a phase of reintegration at the Invalides, in which he joined the company of other illustrious French soldiers.[35] The Parisian itinerary of the procession was similar to that of the return of Napoleon's ashes in 1840 – another aspect of the ceremony that underlined de Lisle's military side. However, the legendary figure of the Emperor dominated his second burial from beginning to end, while de Lisle's unique personality gradually merged with his song.

De Lisle's body was ceremonially exhumed on 13 July at the cemetery of Choisy-le-Roi, in the presence of local and national officials, and then was brought to the municipality in a solemn procession, accompanied by military units, and delegations of war veterans and boy scouts. In the ceremony at the municipality he kept at first his individual traits, as the mayor recalled his miserable old age, the local citizens' attempts to help him, and the refuge he had finally found in that small town. However, the other orator, the Minister of the Interior Malvy, shifted the emphasis to the matter in hand: he expressed the nation's gratitude to the writer of the national anthem, and compared the soldiers of 1793 with contemporary combatants, both of whom fought to the sound of the *Marseillaise*.[36] The coffin was afterwards presented to the general public in a magnificent red and gold catafalque – another sign of de Lisle's new status.

Next morning, on its way to the Arc de Triomphe, the coffin and its military escort passed through Place de la Concorde,

35. For the structure of a rite of passage, see Victor Turner's elaboration of the model suggested by Van-Gennep, in *The Ritual Process: Structure and Anti-Structure*, Ithaca, Cornell University Press, 1977, pp. 94-97.

36. See *Le Temps*, 15 July 1915 and *Le Figaro*, 15 July 1915 for the details of the ceremonies at Choisy-le-Roi and Paris.

where they were greeted by a large crowd of the *Ligue des Patriotes*, led by its president, Maurice Barrès, which had just participated in a commemorative ceremony in front of the allegorical statue of Strasbourg. The fact that the *Marseillaise* had been composed in that city, which had been occupied by the Germans since 1870, made this encounter especially poignant. In the Arch, the coffin was transferred to a gun carriage from the time of the French Revolution, covered with tricolour flags, and was placed under Rude's relief, depicting the departure of volunteers to war, and associated with the *Marseillaise*.

The ceremony began with the singing of the anthem by two opera singers, and continued with a solemn procession through the Champs-Elysées in which President Poincaré, Prime Minister Viviani, the government, the parliament, all the civil and military authorities of the State, military units and delegations of school-children all participated. The enormous crowd of spectators, made up mainly of women, children and old people, was dense, and many among them wore medals with the symbol of the city of Paris and a portrait of de Lisle, sold for the benefit of the war effort.[37] A novelty, which subsequently became a common sight in such cere-monies, was a formation of aeroplanes that flew low above the pro-cession, giving a symbolic escort to the coffin and also serving as cover in case of German aerial attack. The general mood was of 'imposing gravity, calm resolution, and patriotic faith.'[38]

The third phase of the ceremony, at the Invalides, consisted mainly of a speech by Poincaré, which he gave standing close by the coffin in the courtyard of the monument. The speech, which was later reproduced on a poster, was a formidable amalgam of a his-tory lesson, a political discourse, and a call for war.[39] The President began by defining the aim of the ceremony as not only marking the memory of the officer who had expressed 'the eternal soul of the fatherland,' but also as bringing closer 'two great pages of our his-tory' through a celebration of the song that was 'a cry of vengeance and indignation of a noble people... which proudly refused to bend before the foreigner.' Poincaré proceeded to offer a brief biographi-cal portrait of de Lisle, and an appreciation of his 'immortal song', and then turned to the present situation. He described the 'military

37. Parisians were invited to watch the ceremony by newspaper notices and posters that included details of the event. *Archives de la Seine, série VK3-187.*

38. *Le Temps,* 15 July 1915.

39. For the text of the speech, see *Journal Officiel de la République Française,* 16 July 1915, pp. 4,838-39. For the poster, see *Archives de la Seine, série VK3-187.*

imperialism' of Germany and Austro-Hungary, rejected the possibility of a 'precarious peace' which would not 'make France whole again', and concluded with a call for a unity to all the provinces, classes, and parties, announcing that 'the glorious day that the *Marseillaise* celebrates is already lighting up the horizon.' The ceremony ended as it had begun, with the singing of the national anthem by the singers and choir of the Opera, joined by the attendant dignitaries and the dense crowd. As usual with public singing, it was a moving demonstration of social cohesion, but this time the song was both the means and the end of the celebration. In the afternoon, and on the morrow of the ceremony, the public, including groups of schoolchildren and war veterans, was allowed to pass in front of the coffin, before it was transferred to its permanent location in the Invalides. The entire event was thus an effort at effacing various distinctions – between the past and the present, the composer and his song, the battle front and the home front, the elite and the people, all in the name of the fatherland.

It is impossible to measure the exact impact of the ceremony, but there is no doubt that the organisers were correct in choosing the *Marseillaise* as a mobilising theme, since the anthem featured widely in different media throughout the war. Three books were published on the anthem and its writer, their authors associated with different components of the Sacred Union: the radical Julien Tiersot, who published a re-edition of his 1892 book, the monarchist Louis de Joantho, and the moderate-republican Louis Fiaux.[40] The Opera presented the 1792 'lyrical scene' by Gossec and Gardel, *The Offering to Liberty*, in which the Revolutionary hymn occupied a central place, and Edmond Rostand recited on the same stage his poem *The Flight of the Marseillaise* (1917). Also, in the numerous patriotic songs and pieces of music that the war inspired, reference to the song was almost obligatory. The *Marseillaise* was heard at the front as well, as it was chanted by combatants facing the enemy, encouraging themselves with memories of the Revolutionary wars. Yet, as the war policy of the regime grew more and more controversial, notably after 1917, so did the *Marseillaise*. It was parodied, replaced at times by the more tender *La Madelon*, and even attacked by the socialists as too bellicose.[41]

---

40. Julien Tiersot, *Histoire de La Marseillaise*, Paris, Delgrave, 1916; Louis de Joantho, *Le Triomphe de La Marseillaise*, Paris, Plon, 1917; Louis Fiaux, *La Marseillaise, son histoire dans l'histoire des Français depuis 1792*, Paris, Fasquelle, 1918.

41. See Vovelle, 'La Marseillaise', pp. 127-31.

After the end of the war, with the break-up of the Sacred Union and the growing polarisation of French society, the national anthem no longer represented any consensus. Whereas the leagues of the extreme Right adopted it as their song, the Communists denounced it as a bourgeois, militarist and colonialist creation, in contrast to the *Internationale* of the working class. The advent of the Popular Front, the 1936 governing coalition of radicals, socialists and Communists, put the *Marseillaise* back at the centre of the political arena. It represented the new alliance in various civic festivals, and was even the main inspiration of Jean Renoir's film about the volunteer armies of the French Revolution, *La Marseillaise* (1937). It regained its Revolutionary dimension, but continued at the same time to be a patriotic song, thus representing different things to different people.

And what about Rouget de Lisle? The Revolutionary artist-soldier who was put in the limelight on 14 July 1915 did not stay there for long. During the war, his image kept appearing in various publications, such as the poster celebrating the 1918 conquest of Strasbourg, in which he was portrayed singing the *Marseillaise* in the familiar gesture of Pils, leading the French army onward. The day after the armistice, Deputy Albert Dalimier, who had been Undersecretary of State for Fine Arts in 1915 and responsible for the ceremony, proposed in the Chamber to make amends and bring de Lisle to the Pantheon. The bill was transferred to the Education and Fine Arts Committee, which turned it down.[42] After the war, the Pantheon seemed too 'leftist' and not patriotic enough, especially with Zola's body in its crypt, and the new military hero, the Unknown Soldier, was buried in 1920 under the Arc de Triomphe. The simple soldier of the people, *le poilu*, thus became the symbol of the victorious French army, and the heroes of the distant past, so necessary during the uncertain period of the war, were pushed aside. De Lisle was 'resurrected' again on the occasion of the centenary of his death in summer 1936, which coincided with the triumph of the Popular Front. Two official commemorative ceremonies were held on 28 June 1936: one at Choisy-le-Roi,[43] another at the Invalides. In addition, his portrait was carried in the

42. *Journal Officiel de la République Française, Documents, 13.11.1918,* p. 1,812.

43. The municipal ceremony at Choisy-le-Roi became the subject of a fierce quarrel between Communists and republicans. See Sylvie Rab, 'La Commémoration du centenaire de la mort de Rouget de Lisle : Choisy-le-Roi, en juin 1936', in *Les Usages Politiques des Fêtes aux XIXe-XX Siècles,* eds Alain Corbin, Noëlle Gérôme and Danielle Tartakowsky, Paris, Publications de la Sorbonne, 1994, pp. 291-304.

14 July procession in Paris alongside the portraits of Eugène Pottier and Pierre Degeyter, the writers of the *Internationale*. It was a sign that the workers' anthem had joined the *Marseillaise* as a symbol of the regime; likewise, de Lisle was no longer alone in the gallery of ancestral poets.

3

THE IMAGE AND MYTH OF THE 'FIFTH COLUMN' DURING THE TWO WORLD WARS

Christian Delporte

> From the Meuse to the Mayenne, from the Ardennes to the Gironde, invisible enemy troops marched in front of the Wehrmacht tanks and cleared the way for them. (...) (This army) was everywhere: from Dunkirk to Marseilles, from Belfort to Brest; from North to South, from East to West.

This quotation is taken from a small book which appeared in 1946, coauthored by a battalion commander in the east during the Débâcle, bearing the unambiguous title: *The Fifth Column*.[1] As far as the author is concerned, there can be no doubt: France lost the war in 1940, betrayed by 'a Machiavellian octopus' with which the enemy infiltrated French territory. As a result, all becomes clear. Why did that bridge not blow up? Because it was cleared of mines by the Fifth Column. Why was such and such a train shunted in the wrong direction? The Fifth Column again! Why did that military store catch fire? The Fifth Column! Of course the blinkered view of that officer, a hero of the 1914-18 war, incapable of understanding how the army reputed to be the most powerful in the world could have collapsed so suddenly, might give rise to a smile. However he shows the strength of a

---

1. Commandant B... and Marcel Cossart, 1939-1940. *La Cinquième colonne*, n.p., Montdidier, 1946, p. 87.

myth which continued to be maintained long after the end of the Second World War.[2]

The theme of the Fifth Column is characteristic of the Phoney War in 1939-40. That is what popularised a phrase first used during the Spanish Civil War (*quinta columna*), in November 1936, when the nationalists, preparing to attack Madrid, announced on the radio that the capital would be taken by five columns: four advancing along the four main roads leading to Madrid, and the fifth formed within the town itself by the partisans of Franco. As early as 1936, the phrase was translated, especially into English and French, to indicate the enemy within, underground and spy organisations operating from within on behalf of the enemy.

However, while the expression was adopted during the Phoney War, the theme itself was already present as early as the First World War. It was born along with propaganda, which opened up the war on a new front with the weapons of psychological warfare. While the written word contributed to developing the myth, images played a large part in illustrating it, establishing its existence and its material nature. To give a comprehensive picture of the subject, proof should be based on the many graphic forms of the mass media in which myth became manifest (e.g., films, postcards, stickers, etc.). We shall restrict ourselves here to examining two, posters and cartoons, seized upon from one war to the next, by the phenomenon of propaganda.

Roots: the Great War

It is well known that French opinion – as the Dreyfus affair showed us – was sensitive to matters of espionage long before the Great War. Denunciation of German espionage and that of Germany's accomplices was, in the prewar years, one of the strongest pillars of nationalist propaganda. From the beginning of the conflict, the senator for the Manche, Gaudin de Villaine, regularly questioned the Minister of the Interior, Malvy, on Government laxity with regard to German espionage in France, and endeavoured to count the number of Germans or nationals from Germany's allies still present on French territory.[3] In the spring of

2. It will be remembered, in particular, that in 1970 Max Gallo wrote a book (published by Plon, Editions Pierre Téqui) entitled: *Cinquième colonne, 1930-1940. Et ce fut la défaite.* ...

3. See M. Gaudin de Villaine, *L'Espionnage allemand en France, 1914-1916*, Paris, Editions Pierre Téqui, 1916.

1915, Jacques Dyssord published a book with the evocative title *L'Espionnage allemand à l'oeuvre* (German Espionage at Work).

Espionage is considered an essential weapon of modern warfare. At the battle front and on the home front images spread this idea widely, in two different ways. At the front, illustrated propaganda called to mind listening and enemy information. As early as the beginning of trench warfare, at the end of 1914, posters warned French soldiers: 'Watch out. The Boche is listening to you' and showed a German (the stereotype with the spiked helmet made famous by caricature), crouching in one corner of the picture, plugging into the field telephone wire through which two French soldiers are communicating, and meticulously taking note of the whole conversation. The silhouette is deliberately just a sketch (by definition, spies are not seen) but the message has the merit of clarity.

Particularly interesting for our research is what happened on the home front, where espionage took on the face of the enemy within, the enemy who had infiltrated France. That is what Alexandre Millerand, the Minister for War, was aiming at when, on 29 October 1915, he published a circular (widely distributed in the press) giving the order that posters (28 x 38 cm) should be put up in all public transport vehicles with this simple text: 'Be quiet. Watch out. Enemy ears are listening to you'. One hundred thousand posters were made available immediately, and preparations were already in hand for a reprint. These posters were to be found in the metro, trains and trams, and also in station waiting rooms; and, gradually, in other public places. Eventually no-one setting foot in town could be unaware of their existence. They haunted daily life, and became so famous that they were sometimes used as slogans for commercial advertising.[4]

These posters came at a period when, in spite of worsening difficulties in daily life and increased prices, French morale remained high, as Jean-Jacques Becker has shown.[5] They appeared especially at a time when the Government wished to mobilise public opinion. German espionage was not the only problem. It was essential to prevent impatience and to justify a meticulous censorship which was precisely controlled by the War Ministry and

4. For example this advertisement for three films at the Omnia-Pathé cinema: 'Impatient civilians, watch the Omnia films, listen to its famous orchestra conducted by Laporte; and be quiet… but here, don't be suspicious, because you can go to the Omnia in all confidence' (*Le Journal*, 20 November 1915).

5. See especially Jean-Jacques Becker, *Les Français dans la Grande Guerre*, Paris, Laffont, 1980; *La France en guerre*, Bruxelles, Complexe, 1988.

which was beginning to weigh heavily. Finally, and above all, it was essential to mobilise the home front with a view to launching the first national loan planned for November 1915. Thus the theme of 'enemy ears' determined the common attitude of the battle front and the home front, united in the same vigilance.

Illustrated official posters were still few and far between during the Great War, when text posters were favoured,[6] and we have found few which enrich the myth under consideration. On the other hand, cartoons were a powerful means of propaganda about the enemy who had infiltrated France, whether expressed in a serious form or humorously. For instance, at the end of 1915/beginning of 1916, caricature took over from the Millerand circular in three ways. First of all, cartoons justified and showed the reality of German espionage. In the columns of *L'Opinion*, 12 January 1916, Forain created this dialogue which he set within an enemy trench: 'We'll have to resign ourselves, we're no longer going to Paris', a German soldier, greatly vexed, is saying. Another immediately replies: 'Yes we are – as spies'. The despondent faces of the soldiers strengthens the substance of the message: German defeat on the ground is inevitable. The only way to reverse the situation is to eat away at France from within, by seeking to win the war in the most despicable way possible, through espionage. In short, the danger is not coming from the front, but from behind the lines.

Next, caricature subverted the message of vigilance for antiparliamentary ends. The scene depicted in 1915 by George-Edward takes place on the floor of the Chamber. A deputy is suddenly stopped in the midst of his verbal flow by the hand of the President of the session, pointing to the Millerand circular on a wall (Figure 3). The cartoonist wonders, 'Why not stick it up in the Chamber as well?'[7] The 'Be quiet' of the circular is thus used to demand silence from the deputies whose inopportune gossip would threaten national cohesion or delay the victorious outcome.

However it must be stressed that these two types of cartoon are not the most frequent. Graphic production on this theme was dominated above all by comic variations around the need to observe silence. Among other examples, we will cite one provided by the special edition which the satirical weekly *La Baïonnette* devoted, on

6. See Laurent Gervereau, *La Propagande par l'affiche*, Paris, Syros-Alternatives, 1991.

7. George-Edward, 'La circulaire Millerand', *L'Oeuvre*, 4 November 1915.

LA CIRCULAIRE MILLERAND

Pourquoi ne pas l'afficher aussi à la Chambre ?

Figure 3 *George-Edward, 'Why not stick it up in the Chamber as well?', 1915*

13 January 1916, to the theme 'Be quiet! Watch out!' (Figure 4). In a street in Montmartre (which traditionally served as the backdrop for the imagination of its creator, Francisque Poulbot), an old man with a frail silhouette, wearing around his neck a notice 'I am deaf and dumb', is being dragged away, with a firm hand, by two strong police officers, watched by a hostile crowd. The bogus deaf-mute is trying in vain to defend himself, yelling to anyone who will listen to him: 'I am naturalised... I am English... I am...'. Finally, the caption gives the reasons for the arrest: 'He was telephoning from the tobacconist's'. The cartoon, apparently without any great pretensions, obviously raises a smile. However, behind the burlesque an appeal for vigilance by the population, for cooperation between the population and the police to expose the enemy, should be noticed. The naive artist Poulbot who, before the War, had confined himself to drawing the street urchins of Paris, owing to the War became a fierce patriot. His anti-German drawings often verged on the most crude propaganda (as is shown by his sketches on enemy atrocities with the caption: 'hands cut off'). Here the cartoon, even in a joking way, plays a part in interiorising the mes-

Figure 4 *Poulbot, 'He was telephoning from the tobacconist's', 1916*

sage: let us beware, there are spies among us; and that is the main point. It is a joke, but never denies the existence of an enemy within, in spite of his insubstantial nature.

The theme returned in 1917 when the enemy within suddenly took on the features of pacifist deputies. The spy was finally revealed: he was not German but French; he was called Malvy or Turmel.[8] There was therefore good reason to watch out. The mixture of pacifism-defeatism-treachery-espionage was widely used from then on by cartoonists. It allowed Forain to reactivate the antiparliamentary caricatures. For instance the cartoon which he drew for *Le Figaro*, entitled *'La séance fut secrète'* (The Session was Secret). An anonymous deputy (as is shown by the distant silhou-

8. In 1917, the radical-socialist permanent Minister of the Interior, Louis Malvy, had been accused by his political opponents (Georges Clemenceau and Léon Daudet in particular), of protecting anarchists and antimilitarists (including Almeyrada, director of the newspaper *Le Bonnet rouge*, imprisoned for contact with the enemy), and even of having informed the Germans at the time of the offensive of the Chemin des Dames and encouraged mutiny in the French Army. Forced to resign on 31 August 1917 and brought before the High Court, he was sentenced to be banished for five years for abuse of authority, in August 1918, although the most serious suspicions about him had been allayed. As for Louis Turmel, a radical-socialist deputy, he was imprisoned, in September 1917, after bringing back from Switzerland more than 300,000 francs whose origins were suspect.

ette of the Palais Bourbon, the French National Assembly, which can be seen on the horizon), perched on the corpses of French soldiers, joins the German lines, and throws to the advance units of the enemy army numerous leaflets containing the text of recent secret deliberations of the Chamber; a distressing cartoon, and yet repeated many times.

The Great War firmly established in people's minds the myth of what was not yet called 'Fifth Column'. At the same time the war played a part in fuelling the rhetoric of treason, already visible in Nationalist iconography from the Dreyfus affair.[9] Talk about traitors did not die out with the advent of peace. Right-wing and extreme Right-wing cartoons were to develop it methodically in the interwar period, from anti-Germanism first of all, through anti-communism, xenophobia and finally anti-Semitism. The extreme Right-wing caricaturists would not rest until they revealed the enemy within: Aristide Briand, representative of Germany at the Quai d'Orsay, the French Foreign Office; Léon Blum who worked first for Germany, then for Stalin; the Communists, Freemasons, political refugees, Jews, etc. France was being eaten into from within by forces which were more or less secret. This was an ever-recurrent theme in newspapers such as *Gringoire* or *Je suis partout* from the time of the Popular Front, as in this cartoon by Phil, dated 1939. The scene takes place on the backstairs of the Soviet Embassy. The place is not explicitly indicated, but we see, framed in the doorway, two people talking. One of them is wearing a *shapka*, a fur hat, embossed with the red star. And while a spy is moving away, his face completely hidden by the collar of his overcoat, the first is saying to the second: 'He's a rogue, but with a conscience. As he takes his payment he always shouts: Long live France!'.[10]

Propaganda through the images used in these newspapers, by methodically developing the rhetoric of subversion, by systematically fuelling fears, prepared the public to believe in the existence of a Fifth Column which had supposedly invaded France. Especially as, during the Phoney War, the enemy was not only German. He was also Communist. He was, according to the wording of the period, *Hitléro-stalinien*. Left-wing cartoons were not to be outdone, denouncing the Fascist plot, the agents of Germany (La

---

9. See Christian Delporte, 'Images d'une guerre franco-française : la caricature au temps de l'affaire Dreyfus', *French Cultural Studies* (June 1995)·221-48.

10. Phil, *Je suis partout*, 23 June 1939.

Rocque, Doriot) and exploiting the Cagoule[11] affair (*Cagoulards* were agents of Mussolini).

In Full Flower: The 'Phoney War'

Seen in the light of 1914, the war which began in 1939 brought with it the slogans of the Great War. For example a poster, printed in Autumn 1939, declared: 'LET'S WIN THE WAR OF NERVES!...' and, like twenty-five years earlier, 'LET'S BE QUIET! LET'S WATCH OUT! Enemy ears are listening to us!...' As proof of the watering-down of propaganda at the time, the document was not issued by the General Commissariat for Information (headed by Jean Giraudoux),[12] but by an agency answerable to the Ministry of the Interior, France-Propagande-1939, situated a short distance from the Place Beauvau, at 4 rue d'Aguesseau. Its small size (close to that of the Millerand poster) indicated that it was to be put up in public places. It was surrounded by a red, white and blue border, which reinforced its official nature. A text poster, it included only one graphic element, but it was a strong symbol: the national flag floating proudly in the wind. The combination of blue (the colour of the printed letters), white (the background of the poster), and red gave its full patriotic weight to a slogan which explicitly repeated that of 1915. About twenty years after the end of the Great War, the slogan of the Millerand circular continued to resonate in the French imagination. The very title 'war of nerves' strengthened the dramatisation of the message and extended the field of armed conflict which, deprived of apparent battles, was also to be won on a psychological level. The first person plural was also used: for '*vous*' (you), was substituted the more collective 'we'. It was not only a question here of solemnly appealing to the

11. Nicknamed '*La Cagoule*', the *Comité secret d'action révolutionnaire* (CSAR – the Secret Committee for Revolutionary Action) was a secret organisation, founded by Eugène Deloncle in 1935. Formed from extreme Right-wing activists, financed by Fascist Italy, the *Cagoule* had given itself the aim of causing a coup d'état which would establish an authoritarian regime of the Mussolini type. Responsible for several murders (including those of the Roselli brothers, antifascist refugees in France) and assassination attempts, the *Cagoule* was dreaming of a military putsch against the Popular Front when it was broken up in November 1937. Under the Occupation, Deloncle was, in Paris, the animator of the Revolutionary Social Movement, one of the main Collaborationist parties.

12. On this point see: Philippe Amaury, *Les Deux premières expériences d'un 'ministère de l'Information' en France*, Paris, L.G.D.J. 1969.

civic conscience, but of showing that the tiller was in good hands, that at the highest level of the State the struggle was permanent and shared, that France was one.

Taken more as a whole, we find again the double nature of the message recalled above: intended for soldiers and intended for civilians. However, this time, the picture of the enemy listening takes on a more clearly tragic turn, as shown by a worrying poster of 1939, unsigned, in which two words stand out, words which answer each other with fatal inevitability: 'Indiscretions. Repercussions'. The image shows a kind of funnel. At the top: the 'indiscretions': a man, whose face can barely be seen, is sending by telephone information classified as 'secret'. At the bottom, at the other end of the wire, dominating two thirds of the poster, the white crosses of a cemetery are lined up, recalling those commemorating the dead who died in battle in 1914-18 (e.g. the cemetery of Verdun). Such are the 'repercussions' of the lack of prudence.

However, the theme of 'enemy ears' was not, in 1939 or 1940, a simple repetition of the warnings of the Great War. In 1914-18, the authorities were only just discovering propaganda. The soldiers themselves remained very reserved with regard to a tool which had scarcely been tried on a grand scale. Twenty years later, things had changed. The Soviet and Fascist regimes showed that mastering the techniques of information and communication played a vital role in the training of the masses. Such techniques had themselves been perfected. Goebbels was a past master in the art of manipulating radio. Now, airwaves, because they know no frontier, represented a genuine danger. Hence the special – and disproportionate – attention given, from September-October 1939, to the broadcasts by the 'traitor' Ferdonnet on Radio Stuttgart, which broadcast defeatist news on French territory. An irrational fear seized hold of the French. Today we know that they overestimated the importance of broadcasts, which nobody, or almost nobody listened to. It does not matter – in the climate of the Phoney War, Radio Stuttgart had symbolic weight. In a war which was static to say the least, on the home front, people were called on to mobilise and to show unfailing vigilance. Radio Stuttgart justified the fears expressed about the enemy within. Indeed, who was feeding information to the traitors who had gone over to the side of the enemy, if not the Fifth Column who had infiltrated France?

Fantasy, which feeds the written word, is also fuelled by images; for example this full page (anonymous) cartoon, which appeared in the Catholic newspaper *Le Pèlerin*, on the 1 October 1939 (Figure 5).

Figure 5 *Anonymous, 'This is Radio Munich...', 1939*

First of all it repeated and underlined a warning from Giraudoux, who was put in charge of propaganda by the Daladier Government: 'The tranquillity of the country, i.e., its salvation, depends on your calmness and your caution when faced with enemy voices, your intelligence in separating them from the others, and the care you take not to spread them'. Illustrating the subject, a mother and her two children are gathered around the wireless set which, made by 'Bobard's Vox' ('Lying Voice'), is broadcasting deliberately erroneous information: 'Polish atrocities', 'the English are forcing France to make war', 'general breakdown of cars in Paris', etc. Pictures embody the fantasy. For example, some French people (a woman and her children left behind while the husband or the father is at the front), unarmed, innocent, are indeed victims of German propaganda. The caption warns: 'Radio hams, watch out, through the voice of German radio it is sirens or traitors who are speaking to you. ...' A double-edged image, for, while it was likely to mobilise the country against the enemy, external or internal, and against the Fifth Column, whose reality was being stressed, it showed at the same time the devastating power of German propaganda and spoke volumes about the morale of the French, ready to succumb to the 'sirens' of the defeatists. The existence of Radio Stuttgart provoked real panic: the Germans knew everything and had informers everywhere. Official propaganda, through counterpropaganda, was to fuel rumours, fears and gullibility, and cultivate the myth of the Fifth Column. We shall justify our remarks using two examples. The first is a famous poster by Paul Colin entitled: 'Silence. The enemy is eavesdropping on your secrets'. Designed in small format (59 x 38.5 cm), it was issued by the technical and artistic section of the General Commissariat for Information, run by the painter and poster designer Jean Carlu.[13] This organization had been set up to 'design propaganda campaigns based on themes defined by the Commissariat'. It was a question of making available 'the technical and psychological resources of commercial advertising', in the field of both slogans and graphics.[14] To create the poster in question, Carlu spoke to his friend, Paul Colin who, like him, won fame both in commercial advertising and in political posters, on the occasion of the Spanish Civil War (Committee for a Free Spain). The document dates from February 1940, a time when rumours about the Fifth Column were at their height; a particularly distressing month for the French. The difficulties, unrest and doubts in connection with the Phoney War intensified irrational fears and reactions. Far from calming fears, the images strengthened them by bearing witness to the presence of 'enemy ears'.

The phrase takes up the slogan of 1915 while having the originality of an advertising slogan: 'Silence' and 'Secrets', two words accentuated (one placed at the top, the other at the bottom of the poster), which answer each other and rhyme (in French: Silences/Confidences). Of course, the poster was intended for the population as a whole, clearly symbolised by the small tubby man (old, and therefore not mobilised), presented full-face, with his walking-stick and trilby. However the central component is the person seen in profile, leaning towards the ear of the former: the soldier, that is to say the soldier on leave. It is he who is speaking, he who, having come from the front, is confiding in the civilian, the man left behind. He who, by telling the story of his life as a soldier, may let slip a military secret and unwittingly be a source of

13. Born in 1900, Carlu had carried out prewar State advertising campaigns (for the National Defence loans). He had also been the official representative to the United States for the Minister of National Education, then of Commerce.

14. National Archives, F 41-14 (Technical and Artistic Section of the General Commissariat for Information).

information for the enemy. Such was, in any case, the opinion of the Second Bureau which became alarmed, at the time, about the indiscretions of soldiers. To reinforce the message, the author has made great use of all the colours. While the background of the poster is in shades of dark blue, the two people are shown in a glaring light. Perfectly visible, they are vulnerable. The 'enemy who is on the lookout' is reduced to a huge shadow, whose gigantic stature shows the magnitude of this sinister danger. He can only be seen through a shaft of light. However, his movement (he is leaning forward) shows that he is listening. To the anonymity of the face in the darkness is added the ordinariness of the silhouette in which only the following can be seen: the shape of the hat (the same as that of the passer-by) and the ear – by definition the listening ear. Nothing shows that he is a German. This anonymity stresses at least two things: firstly that the enemy is everywhere, then that this enemy is polymorphous (so the theme of the Hitlero-Stalinist enemy resurfaces). It should be added that the poster became so famous that, after the war, Paul Colin reused the composition to launch a text by Jules Romains which was to appear in serial form, in *L'Aurore*.[15]

Another example: a poster showing the serious face of a man, covering his mouth with a red, white and blue gag,[16] with this slogan: 'To be quiet is to serve'. The document is characteristic of the generalisation, of the penetration into daily life of the theme of the Fifth Column. Made by the printer Draeger (who specialised in posters for France itself), it was used as an advert for a famous make of anisette aperitif, launched a few years earlier by Ricard ('offered by RICARD, the real pastis from Marseilles'). The poster attracts our attention on at least two counts. Firstly, it is private propaganda. The commercial approach has joined civic action and shows that mobilisation was general. Advertising both showed the trivialisation of the myth and played a part in establishing it firmly in people's minds. The Fifth Column became a commercial medium. Secondly, it is interesting from the point of view of the

15. '*A partir du 18 janvier, chaque jour dans L'Aurore, Examen de Conscience des Français par Jules Romains, de l'Académie française. Ce qui ne va pas, ce qu'il faut faire. Illustré par Paul Colin*' ('From 18 January, every day in L'Aurore, Examination of Conscience for the French by Jules Romains, of the Académie Française. What should and should not be done. Illustrated by Paul Colin'), poster by Paul Colin (158 x 117), 1947.

16. The features and symmetry are somewhat reminiscent of the pictorial material of Fascist Italy.

places it was intended for, since it was put up on walls or above the counters in bars and 'bistrots', convivial institutions which are typically French, places which favour conversation and exchanges. A place which is uncontrollable by definition. Anyone can go there. You can be listened to by anyone there. The poster was aimed especially at cafés where soldiers and civilians met.

These posters were along the same lines: they showed the idea that the enemy was present at the very heart of all the most common places in daily life. He was in public places, cafés, in the street. He *was* there, even if he could not be seen.

As for humorous cartoons, they too took up the theme of the Fifth Column; for example the plate by Ian Peterson, 'Enemy ears are listening to you...', which appeared in the Fayard publishing house weekly, *Candide*, on 13 March 1940. In nine illustrations, Peterson shows the most absurd situations and places in which agents of Hitler (and Hitler himself, as it happens) might overhear the conversations of the French: in middle-class lounges, during a game of chess; at the vet's; at the cinema; on a race track, etc. And even on a desert island: while a man is preparing to throw a bottle into the sea, his companion warns: 'And above all, in your message, don't put anything which might reveal our position'. At the same time, the reader sees, in the foreground, a mermaid bathing in the water, with a face strangely reminiscent of the Führer. Two decades on, Peterson's composition obviously echoes that of Poulbot mentioned earlier. Beyond the comic variations, it shows us to what extent the theme of 'enemy ears listening to us' was to be found in the world of the French, even more so than during the Great War. While they sought to make fears less alarming, cartoons also stressed to what extent the Fifth Column had become an obsession of public opinion.

So the myth of the listening enemy who had infiltrated France, while having its roots in the Great War, clearly developed in 1939-40, took a more dramatic turn and put the soldier to the fore. Propaganda, by showing the reality of the Fifth Column, prepared people's minds for the idea of a weakened army, eaten into from within. So much so that at the time of the final disaster propaganda about the Fifth Column finally had a 'boomerang' effect. When people wondered about the sudden terrible collapse of the French army, one answer came spontaneously to mind: France had been betrayed from within. The invisible enemy was indeed as effective as had been said. It had broken military resistance and left the population to their own devices.

Revival: The Liberation

The myth of the Fifth Column did not die out with the Occupation and Vichy. It reappeared with a vengeance with the Liberation: firstly, because the hour of reckoning had arrived. It is sufficient to mention the brochure published in 1944 by Albert Bayet (in which he took up a text written during the Resistance), entitled *Pétain et la cinquième colonne*, aiming to show that France, in 1940, had been the victim of a plot led by Pétain, agent of Germany and leader of the Fifth Column.[17] This was at the time of the purge. The collaborators, many of whom were in hiding, were prosecuted precisely for 'contact with the enemy'. Then the theme surfaced again because the war was not over. The battles remained indecisive, morale uncertain, especially at the time of the Ardennes battle (December 1944). People had to remain vigilant: the cunning enemy was still on French territory.

The theme of the Fifth Column was then naturally developed by War Ministry propaganda, for example in the poster by M. Mallet, created at the end of 1944. Against a backdrop of ruins, the shadow of the enemy is stealing away. Just as in 1915, so in 1939, there is an appeal for vigilance and for silence: 'Be quiet. The Germans have fled. The spies remain!'. For, while the Wehrmacht had beaten a retreat, it had left behind it battalions of armed collaborators who, taking advantage of the chaos, wanted to sabotage the revival of France. This presence of the Fifth Column, which falls more into the category of fantasy than reality, justified, in the eyes of some (and especially the Communists who were very much present in the Department for Information), maintaining the patriotic militia. It will be recalled, especially, that the shooting at Notre Dame, on 26 August 1944 (the day when De Gaulle symbolically walked down the Champs Elysées in liberated Paris), had, without the slightest shadow of proof, been attributed to the Fifth Column[18]. The next day, the Communist press and papers with Communist support had called for the reinforcement of the armed militia which the General, anxious to restore the authority of the

17. 'No, France was not defeated: France was sold out. (...) By whom? By a bunch of traitors. Who were that bunch? The Fifth Column. Who was its leader? Philippe Pétain' (Albert Bayet, *Pétain et la Cinquième colonne*, Paris, Société Edition de Franc-Tireur, 1944, p. 12).

18. See Pierre Laborie 'Les manifestations du 26 août' in *Paris 1944. Les enjeux de la Libération*, Paris, Albin Michel, 1955, pp. 377-89.

State, wanted to see rapidly disappear. Thus, the Fifth Column, at the time of the Liberation, became a major political stake.

The myth of the Fifth Column finally faded in the early months of 1945 at a time when the outcome of the war was no longer in doubt and the Republic appeared to rest on firm foundations. One of the last graphic signs was this poster by Mallet (at the beginning of 1945): the same author, the same backer as before and also the same slogan: 'Be quiet. The Germans have fled. The spies remain'. The picture seems frozen: an officer of the Wehrmacht is pricking up his ears (emphasised by a white border) to hear hypothetical information. But what is remarkable here is the origin of the stereotype; the same poster could very easily have been printed during the Great War, so like the classic image of a Prussian officer is the man represented. With his monocle, his shaven head and his straight back, he could easily be taken for Erich von Stroheim in *La Grande Illusion*!

The theme of the Fifth Column reflected the fantasies, fears and doubts of public opinion. It was in 1915 or in 1945 that people dared to show the face of the enemy; not in 1939; not in 1940. The authorities used the theme to allay impatience, as in 1915, to explain the apparent lack of action as in 1940, and to justify the slowness in restoring order as in 1944-45. However in 1918, as in 1945, France was in the victors' camp. In 1940, on the other hand, it was in a state of collapse and the Fifth Column acted as a telltale sign. The theme took hold of public opinion, all the more strongly because for years public opinion had been conditioned by propaganda to fear the enemy within.

It is still difficult to measure the impact of graphic portrayals, even if – as the poster by Colin shows – certain images seem to have had a great effect on public opinion. Let us note only that the iconography of propaganda revives the theme, gives it shape, cultivates it in public opinion.

It will have been noted that pictures scarcely seek to embody the intangible. The spy remains absent or is only shown through a furtive shadow. The image is above all the medium for a slogan. It accepts the presence of the Fifth Column as a genuine fact to address the public-spiritedness of public opinion. The poster presents the message and gives it all its emotional weight. It calls out to the passer-by and orders him to do something which he cannot escape. Even humorous cartoons are involved in this propaganda. While they describe to the point of absurdity the consequences of the slogan, they never question its validity. Let us make clear also that the theme of the Fifth Column, deeply interiorised, did not give rise to any graphic counterpropaganda either in the pacifist press of the Great War, or in the nonconformist newspapers, such as *Le Canard enchaîné*, in 1939-40.

One final remark: while before 1939, France seemed to be at the forefront, she did not have a monopoly on the theme of the Fifth Column during the War. It can be found in the propaganda of all the belligerents, at one time or another, especially when the War is entering a more acute phase or the outcome is becoming more uncertain. Thus two examples can briefly be mentioned which, while they fall into a now familiar category, belong to different registers. The first, British, will remind French readers of a well-known saying, according to which, 'walls have ears'. The poster, signed by Bruce Bairnsfather, dealt with in the form of a caricature, shows two soldiers, one young and one older who, given his age and his decorations, no doubt fought in the Great War. Two generations, that of father and son, find themselves thus joined together in uniform. Yesterday's espionage finds a weighty echo in the war of today, as shown by the backdrop: a stone wall against which a huge ear linked by four wires to a swastika stands out. 'Even the walls...', announces the poster in the upper part, whilst in the lower part, a short dialogue begins. 'S'long Dad! We're shiftin' to...', the younger man starts to say. The older man interrupts him, with a vexed expression, his finger on his mouth. 'Blimey, I nearly said it!'

The other poster, which is German, dated 1943, belongs to a series on the same theme, with the same slogan. In a café, a couple are talking, while a waiter is bringing cups. A huge shadow covers three quarters of the picture: that of a man, no doubt ordinary, as is stressed by the picture of his hat, and therefore all the more remarkable. The short slogan, 'Pst', stressed by an exclamation mark, tells the whole German nation to be quiet in public places.

These two brief examples show how familiar the idea of espionage had become, both at the battle front and on the home front, in both camps, and how rooted in the collective unconscious. They also show that psychological warfare now held a central place in this endless conflict. The Fifth Column, whether called by that name or by some other, is therefore a shared myth of modern warfare. Propaganda imagery, characteristic of the emergence of mass societies, is a powerful indication of this myth.

Translated by Marlene Burt

4

FIGHTING MYTH WITH REALITY

The Fall of France, Anglophobia and the BBC

Martyn Cornick

This study explores some of the key aspects of how the British, through the BBC, fought a propaganda war with Occupied France with the ultimate aim of fostering tacit and active resistance among the population. In order to elucidate the historical context, and to enable a broader understanding of the scale of the task facing the BBC, the first part focuses on the myths underlying Franco-British relations in the period prior to the fall of France. Secondly the nature and agencies of French Anglophobia in the war of words between France and Britain will be examined briefly, and finally the practical ways in which the British countered propaganda will be reviewed to show especially that the correspondence received from listeners to the BBC contains some revealing insights into the nature of everyday existence under the Occupation. Because France and Britain were not actually engaged in combat with each other during the Occupation, save in skirmishes around the Middle East and Africa, for the first two years of the war hostilities between the former allies amounted to a sometimes savage war of words in a struggle to win over public opinion. Following their armistice of 22 June 1940, the Germans and the French, under the leadership of Marshal Pétain – and it should be remembered that the Vichy regime conducted its own propaganda campaigns independent of the occupiers – resorted on an unprecedented scale to the myths of anglophobia in expositions of their policy and propaganda.

Initially attention will be focused on the two powerful myths underlying Franco-British perceptions during the period just before and after the fall of France. These myths are bound up together: they are the 'Myth of the War Experience' (as conceived by George Mosse[1]) and the myth of the Entente Cordiale. Evidence of these may be found in different examples during the 1930s, but here a major instance from the late 1930s will be examined in which the two myths are combined with equal force.

The Myth of the War Experience and the Myth of the Entente

On 19 July 1938, a few weeks before the conclusion of the Munich accords and just over a year before the outbreak of war, King George VI and Queen Elizabeth embarked on a meticulously planned state visit to France.[2] Their visit began with the inauguration of a huge bronze monument named *Britannia* erected at the entrance to Boulogne harbour (Figure 6). Very few people remember this today because it was blown up by the Germans. In an imposing ceremony it was unveiled as the royal yacht *Enchantress* steamed into port. The monument was conceived with two purposes in mind. First, in the historical context of the long-standing relationship between the British and the French port, it commemorated the fact that immediately after the declaration of war in August 1914 the British Expeditionary Force (BEF) had landed and established the British army's first forward supply centre there. Boulogne was a pivotal link in the supply route between Britain and France throughout the hostilities, and as the war went on, countless troops passed through to and from the front; thousands of wounded British and Allied servicemen were hospitalised behind the lines there; finally, more than twelve thousand servicemen died of their wounds and were buried in the British military cemeteries around the town, among the first to be completed after the 1918 armistice.

1. G. Mosse, *Fallen Soldiers. Reshaping the Memory of the World Wars*, Oxford University Press, 1990, especially chapter 1.
2. For a study of the preparations and how the French press treated the visit, see R. Dubreuil, 'La visite des souverains britanniques', in (eds) J. Bourdin and R. Rémond, *La France et les Français en 1938-39*, Paris, Presses de la Fondation Nationale des Sciences Politiques, 1978, pp. 77-94.

Figure 6 *The Britannia Monument at Boulogne, 1938*

The second purpose behind the unveiling of *Britannia*, as reflected in the effusive speeches made at the inauguration ceremony, was to provide a morale-booster to reassure public opinion in both countries that the Entente was still cordial.[3] Moreover, on their homeward journey from Paris the royal visitors stopped off to inaugurate the new Australian war memorial at Villers-Bretonneux. Their visit was therefore intended not only to celebrate Franco-British relations and cement the Entente, it was also inseparably tied to the other mythic element, a phenomenon conceived by George Mosse as the 'Myth of the War Experience'. The potency of this myth, which conferred meaning on the slaughter of the Great War, and implied that another such conflict must be avoided at all costs, would reach its peak by the time of Munich (September 1938), for by this time the French had built some thirty-six thousand monuments to their 1.4 million war dead, officially remem-

3. See the special issue of *France-Grande Bretagne*, no. 178 (July-August 1938), the journal of the United Associations of Great Britain and France. I am grateful to M. Debussche of the Château-Musée de Boulogne for supplementary information on the statue.

bered throughout the land each November. Furthermore, on several occasions during the 1930s, including the royal inauguration at Villers-Bretonneux, the Commonwealth Allies' sacrifice was also commemorated.[4] Yet this is also myth in the sense intended by Roland Barthes, myth as ideology, myth which found ready expression through those who inaugurated the *Britannia* Monument, as well as political commentators and intellectuals.[5] In other words, as far as the early events of the war are concerned (particularly the retreat from Dunkirk and the Royal Navy's attack on Mers el Kébir), these powerful myths masked the deep-seated shortcomings in the relationship between the two allies, weaknesses which were all too apparent in the collapse of France. And as though to underline this Allied collapse, very soon after they occupied Boulogne, almost two years after the statue's inauguration the Germans lost no time in dynamiting *Britannia* on 1 July 1940.

One of those present at the *Britannia* inauguration who gave expression to these combined myths was Marshal Philippe Pétain. Pétain, as the hero of Verdun, was inevitably involved in the articulation of the myth. In his speech at Boulogne, Pétain enunciated a hymn of praise to the Entente.[6] For those engaged in mediating opinion in 1938, there was nothing in this speech to suggest that Pétain was not sincere in his pro-British sentiments. With the luxury of hindsight, however, the text provides a striking contrast with which to underline the forcefulness of the myths in whose context the nature of Franco-British relations need to be considered.

What did Pétain really think of the British? After all, Pétain was present at other such occasions during the interwar period, even travelling to London for a Franco-British Association meeting in 1935.[7] It seems, obviously enough perhaps, that what Pétain said depended on his audience. Caught up as he was in the myth of the war experience, he could appear fully to endorse the Entente with Britain, as in October 1935 or July 1938. But in a conversation with the Italian ambassador, recorded in Paris in February 1936, and unearthed by Philippe Burrin, Pétain revealed what he thought of

4. M. Gilbert, *The First World War*, London, Weidenfeld and Nicolson, 1994, pp. 536-38.

5. For an example see P. Barrès, 'Après la visite du Roi George VI', *Revue des deux mondes* (15 August 1938):918-25.

6. The speech is reproduced at the end of this chapter (above).

7. See *The Times*, 24 October 1935. Lord Cavan, introducing Pétain, was 'thankful that relations with France were of such cordiality that there was no imminent danger of this great fighting Norman following the example of his Norman predecessor in 1066' (ibid.).

the Entente partner, views which clearly anticipate the anti-British stance he would adopt in 1940. 'England has always been France's most implacable enemy', declared Pétain.

> She only waged war at France's side because this served her own interests, and then she backed Germany. For all these reasons, I believe that France has two hereditary enemies, the English and the Germans, but the former are older and more perfidious; that is why I would favour an alliance with the Germans which would guarantee absolute peace in Europe, especially were Italy to join this alliance. If this happened, all those problems which have remained unsolved until now would be resolved, because a more equitable distribution of Britain's colonies would provide wealth and work for all.[8]

Here, in condensed form, albeit expressed in confidence at a time of international tension, is the whole Vichy project as far as relations with Britain and Germany are concerned; it anticipates the policy stance which Pétain, Laval and others would adopt after the fall of France.

Anglophobia and the French Identity Crisis

Some comments about the myths of anglophobia are apposite here. The use of anglophobia as a propaganda theme has a particular relevance in Occupied France because of the sudden ending of the Entente that had linked France and Britain since the First World War. It has further importance because the Vichy period represents, in Pierre Laborie's words, the culmination of France's 'identity crisis'.[9] This crisis has medium and short-term explanations. In the medium term, as Laborie suggests, the cumulative effects of internecine political warfare and confusion during the 1930s undermined the unity of the nation. In the short term, once war had broken out in September 1939, many of those in positions of influence perceived France as having been dragged into a war it had striven hard to avoid by an ally who, in retrospect, so it was argued, had tended to subordinate France's national interests to its own. Certainly Pétain, Laval and Darlan and others among

---

8. 'Conversazione R. Ambasciatore-Maresciallo Pétain', *Affari Politici Francia* 20, Foreign Affairs Ministry Archives Rome, quoted in P. Burrin, *La France à l'heure allemande 1940-1944*, Paris, Seuil, 1995, p. 68.

9. P. Laborie, *L'Opinion française sous Vichy*, Paris, Seuil, 1990.

their entourage believed that France's interests would best be served by the defeat of Britain; they had no hesitation in saying so quite openly in diplomatic circles. Thus Robert Murphy, the United States Chargé d'Affaires in Vichy, recorded several instances of the new regime's thinking: 'he [Pétain] expressed indignation over the brutal selfishness of England. He blamed in large part English disregard and ignorance of the interest of continental countries in its rash declaration of war [...] for the present state of affairs in Europe and France's tragedy' (7 August 1940).

Laval too 'hoped ardently that the British would be defeated' and insisted that 'France had suffered too often as a result of British dishonesty and hypocrisy' (29 July 1940).[10]

Evidence exists to suggest that this was a belief widely held throughout France during the first weeks of the Occupation.[11]

The urgent task during the post-defeat period was to identify those 'enemies' within and abroad who had led France into crisis. In terms of national politics, the perpetrators were the 'corrupt' Third Republic and, more specifically, the leaders of the Popular Front; on the level of international relations, Britain was almost universally seen as the main culprit. Connections were made between the two, an attitude peddled by Vichy apologists, one of whom accused French governments since the Popular Front of being the dupes of a Masonic plot coordinated from London.[12] In order to forge a new identity for France, ties with the Entente partner had to be cut, and the perfidious ally needed to be transmuted back into the hereditary enemy. Familiar anglophobic myths (from Joan of Arc through the colonial and Napoleonic wars to Fashoda and the Boer War) together with reminders of more recent Anglo-French clashes were put to work in an attempt to rally the French population behind Pétain and the policy of '*la France seule*' (France alone).[13] These myths were also central in the propaganda campaigns of the Collaborationists, who eschewed the policy of 'France alone', preferring to see France and Germany unite in their

10. See *Foreign Relations of the US, Diplomatic Papers 1940*, vol. II, *General and Europe*, Washington, Government Printing Office, 1957, pp. 379-80.

11. Apart from the influence of appeasers, defeatists, pacifists and fifth columnists, the success of German propaganda during the 'Phoney War' was a major contributory factor. On all these, see J.-L. Crémieux-Brilhac, *Les Français de l'an 40*. Vol. I, *La guerre oui ou non?*, Paris, Gallimard, 1990, *passim*.

12. See H. Valentino, *Les Anglais et nous*, Paris, Jean-Renard, 1941, 111-12.

13. One such example is the album *Un siècle de perfidies jugé par les caricaturistes français*, Paris, privately published, 1941, reproducing anti-British cartoons from the 1890s and 1900s.

efforts to establish a New European Order as a bulwark against 'international Jewry', bolshevism and Anglo-Saxon (or 'Anglo-American') domination.

In the immediate aftermath of the British attack on the French fleet at Oran, or Mers el Kébir, on 3 July 1940, this policy was triggered when Pierre Laval articulated his justification of future collaboration with the Nazis in exclusively anglophobic terms:

> France has never had and never will have a more inveterate enemy than Great Britain. [...] Our whole history bears witness to that. We have been nothing but toys in the hands of England, who has exploited us to ensure her own safety. Today we are at the bottom of the abyss where she led us... I see only one way to restore France [...] to the position to which she is entitled: namely, to ally ourselves resolutely with Germany and to confront England together.[14]

The French government severed diplomatic relations with Britain. In a speech widely reported in the press, Foreign Minister Paul Baudouin assessed the Anglo-French alliance: for too long French foreign policy had been subordinated to British demands, obstacles had been put in the way of French *rapprochement* with Rome and Berlin; the only way forward was to reassert French independence:

> Let our diplomacy become free at last. It must no longer be a tool of hollow ideologies, nor should it serve the designs of foreign powers. Over the centuries, it was purely because of the independence of her foreign policy that France became a great nation. She will become great again only if she returns to this principle.[15]

Even a liberal intellectual like François Mauriac, in despair at the severing of the Entente after all the heroic efforts to forge it, thus setting centuries of enmity aside, could lament that through the Royal Navy's actions at Oran, 'Churchill has rallied a united France against England for many years to come'.[16] However, after the start of the Battle of Britain, opinion would soon turn in Britain's favour.

Anti-British Propaganda in Occupied France

Dominique Rossignol has shown that the production of propaganda by *all* services (German, Collaborationist and Vichy)

14. G. Warner, *Pierre Laval and the Eclipse of France*, London, Eyre and Spottiswoode, 1968, p. 198.
15. *Le Temps*, 6 July 1940.
16. F. Mauriac, *Le Figaro*, 15 July 1940.

against the 'Anglo-Americans' was the 'most voluminous'.[17] Indeed, from the first days of the Occupation until November 1942, England was virtually the only target for such propaganda. During the first year after the Battle of France, anglophobic myths were supported by three themes: inadequate British support for France leading to the defeat; Britain's perfidy, or treachery; and British designs on the French Empire. Conveniently enough, three events came in close succession during the summer of 1940 to illustrate these themes perfectly, and which thereafter formed the foundations of French propaganda in the war of words: these were Dunkirk, Mers el Kébir and Dakar. The scale of the task facing those in London may be more readily appreciated by rapidly examining each one of these.

Dunkirk symbolised the abandonment of France by Britain. Effective German propaganda, much of it articulated on Radio Stuttgart by Paul Ferdonnet (France's 'Lord Haw-Haw'), for a while gained the upper hand by persuading the French that Dunkirk was the culmination of a series of disasters in which the British had abandoned France to its fate.[18] Explanations and further examples of this were traced to the time of the First World War, and especially to Britain's attitude to France during and after the negotiations over the Versailles Treaty, in which Britain was supposed to have sacrificed the interests of French security in favour of German ambitions. Clemenceau's bitterness towards the peace was at the front of many minds.[19] The débâcle at Dunkirk, then, led directly to the Allied collapse and the fall of France.

The second event was the shelling of the French fleet at Mers el Kébir. Nearly 1,300 French sailors were killed during 'Operation Catapult', a crucial attack about which much has been written.[20] Jean Moulin's biographer holds that it determined the course of the war.[21] Whatever the historical arguments, it is important to remem-

17. D. Rossignol, *Histoire de la propagande en France de 1940 à 1944*, Paris, Presses Universitaires de France, 1990, p. 311.

18. See E. T. Lean, *Voices in the Darkness. The Story of the European Radio War*, London, Secker and Warburg, 1943, pp. 104-41.

19. See G. Clemenceau, *Grandeur and Misery of Victory*, London, Harrap, 1930. Another work alerting opinion to the dangers of following British policy is H. Vibert, *Face à l'Angleterre*, Paris, Baudinière, 1936.

20. Cf. A. Marder, 'Oran 3rd July', in his book *From Scapa Flow to Oran*, Oxford University Press, 1976, and H. Couteau-Bégarie and C. Huan, *Mers el Kébir 1940. La rupture franco-britannique*, Paris, Economica, 1994.

21. D. Cordier, *Jean Moulin, l'inconnu du Panthéon*. Vol. 3, *De Gaulle, capitale de la Résistance*, Paris, Lattès, 1993, p. 161.

ber that *at the time*, for several reasons the British maximised the propaganda value of Oran. At home it was a morale booster, showing off the redoubtable power of the Royal Navy. It also clearly demonstrated Churchill's resolve to fight on even if, for strategic reasons, it meant attacking Britain's former ally. As evidenced by the coverage in the British press, and the reception of his statement to the House of Commons, the attack quickly conferred almost mythical status on Churchill himself.[22] Finally, Oran showed the world – and the President of the United States above all – that Britain would stop at nothing to fight on, alone if need be.

For Vichy and the Collaborationists, Oran provided a convenient reminder from contemporary history of age-old British perfidy. For instance, deliberately timed to coincide with the meeting of Pétain and Hitler at Montoire, on 23 October 1940 the cinema newsreel *Actualités mondiales* devoted 200 metres of film[23] to the incident as though to justify the steps being taken towards Franco-German collaboration. Newspapers received orders from the Information Ministry to commemorate the first anniversary prominently (3 July 1941).[24]

The third event was Dakar. After 23 September 1940, when British and Gaullist forces failed in their attempted landing in French West Africa, every opportunity was taken to emphasise British perfidy and to highlight Britain's designs on the Empire.[25] Indeed, because de Gaulle had already been accused and sentenced in his absence by Vichy for treasonable acts and desertion, the Dakar incident reinforced the message that the Free French and the British were tarred with the same brush. A poster distributed by Vichy in 1942 entitled '*Hier, aujourd'hui, demain?...*' ('Yesterday, Today, Tomorrow?...') (Figure 7) provides a visual shorthand of the main themes and stereotypes invoked by propaganda services in Occupied France. Based on the supposedly irrefutable evidence of history, a greedy British bulldog – a reference both to the historic caricature John Bull and to Churchill himself – is shown trying to swallow up the world to expand its own empire at the expense of French blood and colonies.

22. See *Illustrated London News*, 13 July 1940, and Churchill's speech, 'The Tragedy of the French Fleet' (4 July 1940), in W.S. Churchill, *Into Battle*, London, Cassell, 1941, pp. 239-46.

23. Rossignol, *Histoire de la propagande*, op. cit., p. 307.

24. P. Limagne, *Ephémérides de quatre années tragiques*, 3 vols, Lavilledieu, Editions de Candide, 1987, Vol. 1, p. 198.

25. Ibid., p. 28.

Figure 7 *'Yesterday, Today, Tomorrow', 1942*

The French press, in both zones, ceaselessly targeted the British. In the Occupied Zone, the *Propaganda Abteilung* in Paris controlled the press, with much enthusiastic assistance from the Collaborationists. Some of the dailies and weeklies almost specialised in anglophobia, depending on their political affiliation and on the contributors writing for them. It is worth pointing to one or two of the more vociferous since relatively little is known of them. Pierre Costantini's *L'Appel* was the weekly organ of the *Ligue Française*, founded in late summer 1940 as the Ligue Anti-Britannique. Costantini distributed a poster declaring war on England because of the cowardly betrayal perpetrated at Mers el Kébir. Were the French going to defend the cause of perfidious Albion?[26] This poster points out that it was widely acknowledged that French opinion was already largely pro-British. The daily *Aujourd'hui* printed material by Paul Chack and Thierry Sandre, both of whom published anti-British books.[27] Chack, a prolific author of naval

26. Poster published 1 August 1940, in Bibliothèque de Documentation Internationale et Contemporaine (BDIC), 4°Δ.908.

27. E.g., P. Chack, *Face aux Anglais*, Paris, Editions de France, 1942, and T. Sandre, *Lettres sans humeur à sa Majesté La Reine d'Angleterre*, Paris, Jean-Renard, 1943.

history and historical fiction, had been an official in Jean Giraudoux's propaganda commission after its creation in 1939. He was
one of the most ubiquitous Paris Collaborationists, and dealt in
anglophobia and anti-Bolshevism with equal enthusiasm.[28] Chack
was undoubtedly one of the most enthusiastic Collaborationists,
and he paid with his life at the Liberation.

In the Unoccupied Zone a number of newspapers took a strong
line against the British. Official propaganda sheets like *L'Espoir
français* often referred to inadequate British support for French
efforts before June 1940.[29] *L'Action Française*, the paper which had
done so much to undermine France's republican polity during the
interwar period, moved to Lyon after the defeat, and accused
Britain daily of having always abandoned France in times of need:
'At the very moment when the real nation is finding its feet, London
is pursuing an abominable campaign against the new French State'.
Charles Maurras never tired of apportioning blame to Britain for
France's past ills, and repeated past accusations that it had con-
spired in the Dreyfus Affair.[30] And *Gringoire*, probably the most
anglophobic paper ever produced in France, relocated its production to Marseille; in October 1940 it was still printing almost half a
million copies weekly. Henri Béraud, the most notorious professional anglophobe, continued to pour forth his vitriol, and reprinted
his pamphlet *Faut-il réduire l'Angleterre en esclavage?* ('Should England be Reduced to Slavery?') on 1 August 1940.[31] To coincide with
the signature in late May 1941 of the Protocols of Paris, measures
which extended Franco-German collaboration, Béraud interviewed
Admiral Darlan.[32] At the height of his powers, the Admiral was
convinced that it would only be a matter of time before the Germans crushed the British: this assumption had long since governed
the actions of many in Vichy. Later Paul Chack also contributed a
profile of Darlan. The racialist discourse used reflects how all the
Allies were lumped together with the Soviets as the enemies of the

28. P. Amaury, *Les deux premières expériences d'un «Ministère de l'Information» en
France*, Paris, L.G.D.J., 1969, p. 51, and Rossignol, *Histoire de la propagande*, op. cit.,
pp. 276-85.

29. The Foreign Office's classified *Basic Handbook* on France says that this gov-
ernment-subsidised publication first appeared in the Southern Zone in January
1941. The *Handbook* lists French newspapers in Part IV Section II, and indicates the
extent of their anti-British line.

30. Quoted in *Gringoire*, 3 October 1940.

31. See my article 'Faut-il réduire l'Angleterre en esclavage? A case study of French
anglophobia', *Franco-British Studies*, no. 14 (1992):3-17.

32. *Gringoire*, 30 May 1941.

New European Order. It also shows the deep conviction of some
that close collaboration with Germany was the only way to protect
Europe against invasion by the 'Bolshevik plague':

> Darlan knows that England, if by some miracle she were to emerge
> victorious from the war, would dictate conditions that would be no
> less severe [than German conditions] and which would, at the same
> time, lead to the spread of the Bolshevik plague over the European
> continent and, here in France, the return to power of Jews and
> Freemasons subservient to Anglo-Saxon policy.[33]

In publishing there was a veritable industry of anti-British
works by 'professional' anglophobes, from famous authors like
Chack, Béraud or Maurras to political journalists and proponents
of Franco-German collaboration such as Marcel Déat, Dominique
Sordet, Jean Luchaire and Georges Blond.[34] Others emerged from
relative obscurity to vent their anglophobia.[35] It would be worth-
while in a further study to re-examine these works in order to identify common themes and the nature of the discourses deployed.

As for French radio, the work of Philippe Henriot and Jean
Hérold-Paquis for Radio Paris is well known.[36] Vichy radio –
Radiodiffusion nationale – also contributed anti-British propaganda,
as did a number of 'clandestine stations' such as *Radio-Révolution*,
which appears to have specialised in anglophobia.[37] One problem
for Vichy radio was that its audience came quickly to believe it
was German-controlled; consequently listeners developed a preference for the news programming of the BBC, even if they were
not necessarily pro-British. In his journal Léon Werth, observing

33. Ibid., 12 September 1941.
34. See Marcel Déat's preface to C. Albert, *L'Angleterre contre l'Europe*, Paris,
Denoël, 1941; D. Sordet, *Août 1940: Naissance de l'anglophilie*, Paris, Inter-France,
1943; J. Luchaire, *Les Anglais et nous. L'action britannique contre la France jusqu'au 13
décembre 1940*, Paris, Editions du Livre moderne, 1941; G. Claude, *De l'hostilité à la
collaboration*, Paris, Editions de France, 1941; G. Claude, *La seule route*, Paris, Inter-
France, 1942.
35. For a sample, see M. Alerme, *Les Causes militaires de notre défaite*, Paris, Inter-
France, 1941, and *Stratégie anglaise*, Paris, Inter-France, 1942; P. Allard, *Comment
l'Angleterre fait la guerre*, Paris, Editions de France, 1942, and *Ici Londres*, Paris, Editions de France, 1942; A. Chaumet, *L'Inde martyre*, Paris, Jean-Renard, 1942; J. La
Hire, *Mort aux Anglais! Vive la France*, Paris, Editions du Livre moderne, 1942.
36. Henriot's talks were published in *Ici, Radio-France*, Paris, Editions de France,
1943, and *Et s'ils débarquaient?*, Paris, Inter-France, 1944, and those of Hérold-
Paquis in *L'Angleterre comme Carthage…*, Paris, Inter-France, 1944.
37. See log sheets from January and February 1941, BBC Written Archive Centre,
Caversham. Referred to hereafter as BBC Archive.

that Vichy radio tended to be mentally screened out by listeners 'like the tick-tock of a clock', noted countless occasions when 'everyone in the country' was listening to the BBC. Another attentive listener, the captive former prime minister Paul Reynaud, noticed that because the audience had begun to switch off before propaganda commentaries started, anti-British editorial was suddenly being injected into the middle of programmes.[38] By the autumn of 1943, Collaborationists were admitting they were losing the radio war: in a sheet produced by the Collaborationist *Inter-France* agency that found its way to the BBC, Dominique Sordet, likening London's radio technique to the administering of a narcotic or even addictive drug, ranted that 'Jewish propaganda [in London] has five million loudspeakers in France' through which 'every household is imbibing ever-increasing doses of Jewish alcohol poured out by Anglo-American radio'; one solution he proposed was to confiscate all radio sets.[39]

The BBC in the Radio War: Countering Myth with Reality

To prosecute the war effectively a constant flow of knowledge about the state of opinion in France was indispensable. Because of the need to demonstrate Britain's determination to fight on, the hopes and feelings of the French population had to be carefully nurtured; the French audience had to be convinced. Also, because of the early recognition by the BBC and those who spoke regularly on the French service (*'les Français parlent aux Français'*) that war by radio was very effective in countering propaganda and even in moulding public opinion, audience feedback was an essential element. It was in the BBC's relationship with its French audience that the effectiveness of its efforts lies. The European Intelligence Department, headed by Emile Delavenay, was the organisation responsible for assessing opinion in France.[40]

38. L. Werth, *Déposition, Journal 1940-1944*, Paris, Viviane Hamy, 1992, pp. 73, 113 (and *passim*); P. Reynaud, *Carnets de captivité 1941-1945*, Paris, Fayard, 1997, p.77 (and *passim*).

39. *'La propagande juive dispose en France de cinq millions de haut-parleurs. Faut-il les laisser en activité?'*; BBC Archive.

40. See M. Cornick, 'Interview with Emile Delavenay: the BBC and the propaganda war against Occupied France', *French History* (September 1994):316-54. See also his memoir, *Témoignage. D'un village savoyard au village mondial*, Aix-en-Provence, Edisud, 1992.

There were four principal means used to gather intelligence. First, the French press was collected and analysed. Newspapers of all kinds, including regional titles and weeklies, some of which were microfilmed by British Intelligence in Lisbon, were sent to London along with diplomatic bags and post. Despite delays in receiving this material, it proved useful because the press carried increasing denials of London's news stories by Vichy and Paris: this confirmed that the BBC was getting through to the French public. Second, there was monitoring of all European broadcasts. Radio monitors tuned in to all stations on French territory and produced daily monitoring digests. Again, denials by French radio of BBC stories were a frequent source of encouragement. A third source of information came from interviews with people returning or fleeing from France. These interviews provided first-hand witness material to complement and confirm information from other sources. The Ministry of Information sent the BBC log sheets from the Royal Victoria Patriotic School in west London, a filter for MI5 military intelligence. Delavenay's office then contacted returners to invite them for interview. Between 1940 and 1944, over 500 interviews were conducted; apart from British repatriates, Breton fishermen, Irish priests and English students, a range of political figures were interviewed, as well as writers and diplomats.[41]

Finally, from the declaration of war in September 1939 one of the most important sources was the largely anonymous correspondence addressed to the BBC from listeners in France. This invaluable source, described by journalist Georges Boris as a 'sort of Golden Book',[42] was a means of keeping a finger on the pulse of public opinion. Extracts from the letters were used to compile monthly, then twice-monthly, intelligence reports. They contained a vast amount of information about reception in France, bearing not only on the radio audience and public opinion, but also details affording a deep insight into everyday life under the Occupation, including signs of resistance. It is fruitful to go back to the letters themselves because often they yield up information not included in reports. So important were they that not only did they warrant a short programme on *'Les Français parlent aux Français'* from 7 October 1940, they were also constantly used in Free French newspapers such as Pierre Comert's *France* and other periodicals such as

41. The author is working on a study of these interviews.
42. G. Boris, 'French Public Opinion since the Armistice', *Fighting France*, no. 2, (Oxford, 1942):13.

La France libre or *Gallus*.[43] They were sent from all over unoccupied France, and from the border area between the two main zones. Many of the letters bear the notation 'via British Embassy Lisbon', having arrived in London by the most circuitous of routes; the envelope of a letter from Blois dated 8 May 1941 bears the postmark 'Montreux 15 May 1941'. Such letters were carried across the Franco-Swiss frontier to avoid detection or the censorship.

Analysis of the substantial volume of listener correspondence during the Phoney War laid the bases for the continuing success of the operation after France fell. Microphone announcements inviting French listeners to write to the BBC had produced as many as a hundred letters per day by the end of February 1940. The April 1940 report showed that most listeners' letters originated from the greater Paris area or the Nord, whilst the June report produced a breakdown showing the social background of correspondents.[44] After the armistice and the designation of the Nord-Pas-de-Calais as a 'forbidden zone', the volume of letters received fell away considerably; yet well over a hundred letters per month continued to arrive. One year after the armistice in July 1941, 193 letters found their way to London – 57 from the Occupied Zone and 136 from the Unoccupied Zone.[45] Even after the Occupation of the whole of France in November 1942 they continued to arrive, although the number diminished considerably. Photocopies of correspondence opened by the British postal censorship, and of letters seized at sea from overseas territories to and from mainland France were also used.

The reports summarising the correspondence were widely distributed under confidential seal, including the Ministry of Information, and later the Political Warfare Executive with which the Intelligence Department came to be closely associated. The correspondence was vital in maintaining contact with listeners, for whom the broadcasts from London provided much solace: 'Frenchmen forget their personal worries and are drawn together

43. The first broadcast based on listeners' letters was made on 7 October 1940. See J.-L. Crémieux-Brilhac (ed.), *Les voix de la liberté*, 5 vols, Paris, Documentation Française, Vol. 1, p. 105. From July 1941 Jacques Brunius hosted a programme entitled '*Courrier de France*'.

44. In February 1940, a total of 1,555 letters were received, of which 1,037 (66.6 per cent) were 'middle class' and 241 (15.5 per cent) from 'workers'. Between 1 March and 23 April, 733 arrived, of which 432 (58.4 per cent) were 'middle' and 12.8 per cent from 'workers'. As the Battle of France broke out, between 24 April and 22 May the number of letters fell to 191, with 55 (28.8 per cent) 'middle' and 51 (26.7 per cent) from 'unidentified' listeners; BBC Archive.

45. BBC Archive. See also Lean, *Voices in the Darkness*, op. cit., p. 168.

in a single thought. People gather round their radio sets, seeking and finding strength with which to face the morrow'.[46] Some letters bear the notation 'acknowledged by mike [microphone]' to show they had been referred to on air in a broadcast. This served a double purpose: first, listeners were encouraged to continue listening in case their letter should be acknowledged; and second, the messages demonstrated that dissident voices were being heard and that their opinions mattered. In some cases series of letters arrived from the same correspondent, once their initial contact had been acknowledged, establishing what one summariser called 'valuable contacts with unpaid local correspondents of the BBC'.[47]

Letters from the Unoccupied Zone were read by Vichy censors, but some still reached London. One 'working class' *ancien combattant* (veteran) expressed his sentiments in a forthright manner: 'My greatest pleasure is to listen to the English broadcasts, the only ones in which I can get at the truth and which are not under the jackboot of the Boche'. This letter was opened by the censor who forwarded it to London with his own message added: 'My best wishes to you all, you who have the courage to fight for freedom'.[48] One letter, despatched via Marseille, epitomises the mix of sentiments current in French public opinion at this time: although both pro-Pétain and pro-British, the writer displays a residual anglophobia, tempered with an intense germanophobia:

> In France the immense majority of people, despite the hatred the cowardly attack on Mers el Kébir has inspired, despite everything, wants to see England victorious. If the French gain nothing from this victory, because of the ferocious egotism of Albion, they know nonetheless that they have everything to lose if Hitler wins. [...] The French – embittered, discouraged and disappointed – want to see Britain succeed, but they are not yet convinced it will happen.[49]

Another letter pointed to how Vichy propaganda was fusing anti-British and anti-Semitic sentiment:

> Everyone has placed their faith in an English victory, which is now regarded as certain since the fine and courageous resistance of the British people [in the Blitz]. [...] Everything is being designed to separate the French from the English; the latest most successful invention is this: 'an English victory is the victory of the Jews, there-

46. Boris, 'French Public Opinion', op. cit., p. 13.
47. BBC Archive, report dated 8 July 1940.
48. BBC Archive, letter dated 20 July 1940 from Lyon.
49. BBC Archive, letter dated 29 July 1940.

fore we should not side with them.' Wherever there are too many [Jews], the effect of this is considerable.[50]

This trend is well documented in detail in the summary reports between July and November 1940: just after the armistice, there was a widely felt trust in Marshal Pétain. As time went on, despite the blockade of French ports, despite some punishing RAF bombing and intense anglophobic propaganda, French attitudes became progressively pro-British as the population gained a more realistic understanding of the nature of the Vichy regime. Thus *before* the meeting at Montoire, when Pétain and Hitler shook hands on 24 October 1940, the most frequently recurring piece of advice from France was that London should moderate criticism of Pétain. The reason given was that the Marshal was a hero of France and that he was the only hope the people had. Later, however, correspondents became much more critical, saying that despite the aura surrounding him, Pétain was being duped or manipulated by the likes of Laval and Darlan.[51]

Letters were sent by a wide range of correspondents, including teenagers of both sexes, a good number of women, *anciens combattants*, well-educated professionals such as doctors and pharmacists, and, most significantly, *groups* of people. Summaries show that the BBC was the source they relied upon most for news about the conduct of the war; many witnesses, including Emile Delavenay, confirm that after the armistice French newspapers and radio were 'thoroughly disbelieved' because they were seen as being entirely under German influence.[52] For this reason, shifts in public opinion in Britain's favour can be traced to the unfolding of events in the war, in particular to the way they were reported and commented on by the BBC and its French service: the Battle of Britain is crucial because it restored people's faith and hopes in British efforts.

Most remarkably, as early as September 1940, the monthly report devoted paragraphs to 'Sabotage and passive resistance', reflecting what broadcasters in London had suspected: British tenacity in the face of the Blitz was proving exemplary in France:

> The reaction against the invader is expressing itself in the form of passive resistance and sabotage. Here are opportunities for us to

50. BBC Archive, letter dated 28 October 1940 posted from Casablanca.

51. One listener testified to this shift in opinion at the end of 1941: '[Pétain] is undoubtedly a defeatist, a traitor, sold like those other common traitors Darlan, Pucheu, Doriot, Laval and the other Déats'; Lean, *Voices in the Darkness*, op. cit., p. 149.

52. See also Werth, *Déposition*, op. cit., *passim*, and *The Times*, 11 October 1940.

make the French conscious of their participation in the struggle [...] Radio-Paris indulges in diatribes against women who wear tri-colour ribbons, and abuses those who show that they are 'hysteri-cally attached to Great Britain' by wearing the cross of Lorraine or the emblem of Joan of Arc. Resistance takes other forms: German posters torn in the night, children's jeering remarks to German sol-diers, or the 'silence and dignity' of the middle class. [...]

After a review of the evidence, the following passage sketches out the future role of the BBC:

The BBC is expected to play its part in this movement. It can do so by keeping Frenchmen everywhere informed of what other French-men and other peoples under German rule are doing; by guiding passive resistance and sabotage so as to make them most effective without endangering lives unnecessarily (the motto *'Sabotage sans suicide'*, or 'SSS', has been suggested); and by giving all those who resist the enemy the impression that they are part of an army or secret society working on a definite plan and collaborating in the great task of national liberation. All emblems, gestures and slogans which can add to the reading of news, the impetus of visual appeal and of repetition can find a place in our programmes, can con-tribute to the strengthening of resistance and fulfil the psychologi-cal need for a sense of solidarity of disarmed resistance.[53]

And indeed, turning back to the letters one finds that they reveal an ingenious, practical and humorous spirit of resistance. London learned about people's signs revealing to the initiated their support for the British and the Free French. One eighteen-year-old woman from Cherbourg, describing herself as a 'good friend *des Tommies'*, let the BBC into her secret:

Here, when you have asked us to show a silent sign of support for you, we do it with pleasure because we are happy to mystify the Boche. On King George's birthday, everyone carried a red rose in their buttonhole, on 2 May we all wore a lily-of-the-valley; then all the young people found something new to do. On a piece of green ribbon everyone carried a five- or ten-centime coin with the RF side showing, and for those who asked for an explanation we gave it to them: well, we said, the 'R' stands for Royal, the hole in the centre of the coin represents 'air', and the 'F', Force. It's an emblem of our dear RAF. And every day we find something else to tease the Ger-mans with.[54]

53. BBC Archive, report dated 30 September 1940.
54. BBC Archive, letter dated 4 May 1941.

After the French service adopted the successful 'V-campaign', first devised and tried out in Belgium by one of Delavenay's colleagues Victor Delaveleye, in the spring of 1941 many listeners wrote to say that V-signs had appeared everywhere. One letter from Bourg-en-Bresse reported that the 'Boches have banned the sale of chalk except to members of the teaching profession, who are also responsible for checking pupils' pockets as they leave their classes.' Reports reached London that even in the forbidden zone around Calais, V-signs were sprouting everywhere; in the Occupied Zone, a wine merchant was told to reduce the initial letters in his advertisement *'Vin à Vendre à Volonté'* ('Wine for Sale – as much as you like').[55]

Songs and jingles were an effective way of making an impression on listeners. The jingle *'Radio-Paris ment, Radio-Paris ment, Radio-Paris est allemand'* ('Radio Paris lies, Radio Paris lies, Radio Paris is German'), sung to the tune of *'La Cucaracha'* and broadcast on 6 September 1940, was one of the most memorable.[56] Maurice van Moppès, one of the Free French team in London, penned substitute lyrics and adapted well-known hits. During the worst of the German blitz on London in the spring of 1941, he supplied new words for Charles Trénet's hit *'Boums'* to show that not only had London withstood the worst that the Luftwaffe could throw at it, the RAF was now retaliating against German cities:

> *Mais Boum! C'est en Allemagn' que, Boum!*
> *Hambourg, Berlin font Boum,*
> *C'est la RAF qui passe! [...]*[57]

('But, boom! It is in Germany that, boom! Hambourg, Berlin go boom! It is the RAF going by!...')

These jingles inspired the audience in their own inventiveness. Some sent copies of their own poems and songs, either to castigate collaborators like Laval, or to demonstrate support for the British. One writer sent yet more new words for *'Boums!'* to celebrate the bombing successes of the RAF *in France*:

> *Mais boum! L'avion anglais fait: boum!*
> *Tout avec lui dit: boum!*
> *Et les coeurs français tressaillent! [...]*[58]

---

55. BBC Archive, letter dated 15 July 1941; report dated 21 May 1941.
56. Ed. Crémieux-Brilhac, *Les voix de la liberté*, op. cit., Vol. 1, p. 72.
57. Ibid., p. 228.
58. BBC Archive, letter dated 15 July 1941.

('But, boom! The English aeroplane goes boom! Everything else says boom! And French hearts leap!...')

Some enclosed quasi-political tracts often of the simplest kind, others urged protests to be forwarded to mayors, *préfets* or even to Pétain himself, whilst yet others sent copies of open letters they had addressed to the Marshal, such as one sent from Pau on the very day of his visit there.

Many letters were sent on behalf of groups of people, whether schoolpupils, peasants, teachers, or simply 'a numerous group of Anglophiles'. If a group or community knew that an individual was crossing the demarcation line, they would compose a joint letter for posting on the other side; one Paris factory worker wrote on behalf of his colleagues.[59] One schoolpupil wrote that in his class of twenty-four, only four were for the collaboration, the rest were for the British, except three or four who were pro-Pétain but who hoped for a British victory.[60] In this same letter was enclosed one of the most ingenious examples of the spirit of resistance. The enclosure was a dirty scrap of paper with the instruction 'To be read open then folded in two'. This is 'Collaboration', a poem so composed that it is effectively three poems in one: apparently a hymn to the collaboration, when read folded in two it turns into a pro-British eulogy on one side and a diatribe against Hitler on the other.[61] This bears witness to a ludic dimension of what the BBC called 'passive resistance'.

Judged overall, the letters received by the BBC suggest that for many in France writing was important psychologically: it was a way of assuaging guilt, of pouring out anger and fear, as well as constituting a private act of defiance against oppression.

Conclusion

After the Allied collapse, the defeat of France and the end of the Entente, disasters which derived partly from the myths and misunderstandings of the Entente, the British fought a desperate war of words with Occupied France. The BBC's Intelligence Depart-

59. BBC Archive, letters dated 19 April 1941, from Tarbes; 'a group of female farm workers', 27 June 1941, from the Auvergne; 'Loulou', factory worker, Paris, 14 September 1941.
60. BBC Archive, letter dated 8 May 1941.
61. This was published in the Free French paper *Gallus* in the U.S.A. and is reproduced in H. Rice, *Bibliography of Documents on Wartime France*, Cambridge, Mass., Harvard Co-operative Society, 1942, p. 126.

ment was in the van of this effort, and helped to build up a picture of the direction and composition of French public opinion that was as complete and as realistic as it could be. Jean-Louis Crémieux-Brilhac has written that largely through the character and appeal of De Gaulle, 'Free France' too was 'at once a reality and a myth'.[62] Indeed, the important thing for the wartime BBC was to inject sufficient reality into this myth in order to make the most persuasive case for the Free French and the British. Even during the war, before postwar myths would sweep all before them, André Philip found it was no exaggeration to claim that 'the underground Resistance movement was built up by the BBC'.[63] Raymond Aubrac too, a loyal listener of the BBC and prominent member of the Resistance in Lyon, told Emile Delavenay that it was the 'cement' of the BBC which had held the 'pebbles' of the Resistance together.[64] An examination of the role played by the BBC's Intelligence Department certainly bears out these claims, and it deserves full recognition for its contribution.

Annexe:[65]

Translation of Marshal Pétain's speech at the inauguration of Britannia, 19 July 1938

Field Marshal (Field Marshal Lord Cavan, invited by Pétain to unveil the monument as the royal yacht entered port):

Firstly let me express the joy I feel at seeing you again today before this monument built to the glory of the British army and Empire. We have met each other several times at similar ceremonies and I vividly remember the warm welcome you extended to me when I came to London for a meeting of the Franco-British Association.

---

62. J.-L. Crémieux-Brilhac, *La France libre. De l'appel du 18 juin à la Libération*, Paris, Gallimard, 1996, p. 211.

63. Lean, *Voices in the Darkness*, op. cit., p. 149.

64. 'In spite of the efficiency of the Resistance organisations the latter are 'pebbles' whereas the BBC is the 'cement' which unites the pebbles in one solid block'; Raymond Aubrac, interviewed by E. Delavenay, 22 February 1944, BBC Archive.

65. This text, from a leaflet issued to all troops serving in Kitchener's New Army, ended with an exhortation not included in Pétain's speech: 'In this new experience you will find temptations both in wine and women. You must entirely resist both temptations, and, while treating all women with perfect courtesy, you should avoid any intimacy.'

Today it is my turn to welcome you to this corner of French territory from where on clear days one can see the English coast.

The monument we are inaugurating today at the entrance to the port of Boulogne has been designed to commemorate the arrival of the first British force that landed in France on 12 August 1914.

Boulogne has always been a point of contact for the French and British peoples; it was a favoured town of Dickens who, in Victorian times, gathered an intimate circle of admirers and friends here. It is a place of tourist and sporting contacts, illustrated by the numerous attempts to swim or row across the Channel, as well as the first airborne crossing by Blériot.

Because of its position opposite the English coast, Boulogne gained the great privilege of welcoming the first elements of the British Expeditionary Force as it entered France. Through this action, that day the Entente Cordiale became a living reality.

The news of this event whipped up immense enthusiasm throughout the whole of France.

— ⬖ —

This initial landing on 12 August was followed by the transportation to France of five infantry divisions and one cavalry division. This was the first contingent of the expeditionary force on the continent; it fought in the 'Battle of the Frontiers' and served as the vanguard to Kitchener's armies.

For more than four years, the flow of reinforcements, supplies, evacuees and troops on leave was never interrupted. Ever growing despite the submarine menace, this flow reflected the greatness of your efforts, the intensity of which followed the rhythms of battle.

But the deep surprise, the initial shock of the war which marked the soul of Boulogne and, through it, all of France, was registered by these khaki battalions landing for the first time in France. During these unforgettable days, the general emotion which these new troops were also experiencing was such that this delightful detail was noted by an English observer: the shy Tommies offered to the young French women who were welcoming them the still-fresh flowers given by their fiancées just before their departure. In their own way, were they not heeding the wise counsel given to them by Lord Kitchener?:

> Remember that the honour of the British army depends on your individual conduct. It will be your duty not only to set an example of discipline and perfect steadiness under fire but also to maintain the most friendly relations with those whom you are helping in this

struggle... You are sure to meet with a welcome and to be trusted; your conduct must justify that welcome and that trust.[66]

The history of the war has shown just how much Field-Marshal Lord Kitchener's advice was heeded.

General Spears has noted that for the first time on French soil, the French soldier could respond to the call of a British sentry with this rallying cry: 'Friend'! We hope firmly now that this will be maintained during our peacetime relations.

From now on all shipping entering the port of Boulogne will pass in front of this monument, recalling the memory of 1914.

Field Marshal, it is a great pleasure for the government which I represent, as it is for all the French people, to know that the first ship to pass, after you have unveiled the monument, will be the one bringing your gracious Sovereigns to France. The first thing their Majesties will see on entering our country will invoke a noble memory and at the same time will offer proof of the profound gratitude of the French people.[66]

(All translations from the French are the author's. I am grateful to Jacqueline Kavanagh for permission to quote from papers in the keeping of the BBC Written Archive Centre at Caversham, and should like to thank the staff there for their assistance in my researches.)

66. Source: *France-Grande Bretagne*, no. 178 (juillet-août 1938).

5

PÉTAIN AND DE GAULLE

Making the Meanings of the Occupation

Christopher Flood

Introduction

Pétain's wartime speeches have been examined extensively by historians and biographers. The same is true of de Gaulle's. But the relationship between the two sets also deserves attention, since Pétain and de Gaulle were competing with each other for the trust and allegiance of the same primary audience, the French people. This chapter compares the myths which they produced in their public discourse as they constructed antagonistic, but symmetrical interpretations of the Occupation in order to support their rival claims to national leadership.[1]

1. The editions used for this chapter are P. Pétain, *Discours aux Français, 17 juin 1940-20 août 1944*, ed. J.-C. Barbas, Paris, Albin Michel, 1989; C. de Gaulle, *Discours et messages*. Vol. 1. *Pendant la guerre, juin 1940-janvier 1946*, Paris, Plon, 1970. As far as I am aware, these are the most comprehensive collections of the wartime speeches (123 texts for Pétain from June 1940 to August 1944, 178 for de Gaulle over the same period), although they do not claim to be complete. Page references to these works are given in the text using abbreviated forms: for Pétain's *Discours aux Français (DF)*, and for de Gaulle's *Discours et messages (DM)*.

For valuable discussions of central themes in the speeches, see, for example, J. Touchard, *Le Gaullisme, 1940-1969*, Paris, Seuil, 1978, pp. 51-69; G. Miller, *Les Pousse-au-jouir du Maréchal Pétain*, Paris, Seuil, 1975. For the wider context of the propaganda war, see, for instance, H. Eck (ed.) *La Guerre des ondes. Histoire des radios de langue française pendant le Deuxième Guerre mondiale*, Paris, Armand Colin, 1985; Bibliothèque de Documentation Internationale Contemporaine, *La Propagande sous Vichy, 1940-1944*, Paris, BDIC/La Découverte, 1990; M. and J.-P. Cointet, *La France à Londres, 1940-1943*, Brussels, Complexe, 1990.

Strictly speaking, the apparent neatness of pairing Pétain and de Gaulle as wartime speechmakers is something of an illusion. Pétain's speeches should perhaps be described as 'Pétain's' in inverted commas. Unlike de Gaulle, the Marshal was not usually the sole author of his own words. Pétain retained the technique which he had used for producing his speeches, articles, and books during the interwar years. As Richard Griffiths puts it in regard to that earlier period, Pétain 'would enounce ideas, his "writers" would clothe them in words, and he would then "correct" the style and content'.[2] Pétain's wartime speeches were collective productions involving one or more members of his entourage – the most frequent contributors being Henri Dumoulin de Labarthète, Yves Bouthillier, Admiral Fernet, General Laure, Dr Bernard Ménétrel, Pierre Caziot, and Henri Massis.[3] Among the many ironies which marked the opposition between de Gaulle and Pétain was the fact that de Gaulle himself had served as one of the Marshal's ghostwriters during the mid-1920s, and that a disputed issue of authorship was among the factors which had led to the growing rift between them in 1927-28, followed by coolness in their contacts before a further break in 1938 on a further question of authorial attribution. Be that as it may, for convenience of reference in the present chapter, I will treat Pétain's speeches as if he were their sole author.

It has often been said that de Gaulle and Pétain were mythmakers. This is true, on condition that the notion of mythmaking is not reduced to the assumption that a myth is simply a widely held but untrue belief, or a quasi-historical but untrue narrative of events. The concept of political mythmaking can be more usefully defined in a neutral, technical sense to refer to the production of discourse with a narrative dimension which purports to offer an accurate account of a set of past, present or predicted political events, but which lends support to, or implies an ideological argument.[4] By virtue of its teller's selection and interpretation of the events recounted, the story has a didactic, exemplary function insofar as it 'demonstrates' the validity or invalidity of a particular set of political values, beliefs and goals of action. For analytical purposes, the question of whether the narration of any such story includes false factual claims, or excludes true facts which would tend to discredit

2. *Marshal Pétain*, London, Constable, 1970, p. 347.

3. See J.-C. Barbas, 'Introduction', in Pétain, *Discours*, pp. 15-53.

4. See C. Flood, *Political Myth: A Theoretical Introduction*, New York, Garland, 1996, for extended discussion of all of the points outlined in this section.

the teller's interpretation of events is obviously not irrelevant, but it is subordinate to the larger issue of ideological colouring.

In the discourse of politicians and overtly partisan commentators narration is very commonly preceded by, interspersed with and/or followed by explicit ideological argument. In other instances, such as scholarly writing which purports to be objective, explicit ideological argument may be minimal or absent, but an ideological message may nevertheless be conveyed by the structure and content of the narrative, descriptions of protagonists and correlation of the outcome of the story with the personal qualities and ideological orientations of the actors.

Political myths cater to the morally satisfying assumption that, although there can be exceptions, good beliefs are generally held by good people who therefore pursue good objectives, act in good ways, form good associations, and create good institutions. Indeed, rather like a religion, an ideology can be shown to be redemptive by bringing out the goodness which had been lost or merely latent in people who had previously been thinking and acting wrongly according to the value system of the ideology in question. Mythopoeic political narratives characteristically show individuals or groups engaged in (re)discovering ideological 'truth' or struggling for the triumph and implementation of ideological 'truth' which they already possess. Mythopoeic stories also offer counter-examples of political/historical actors who defend false beliefs, or at least fail to acquire understanding of ideological truth. Because it is natural to assume that good ought to triumph over bad and right defeat wrong, it is no less natural to imagine that those who embody the good *must* eventually succeed in achieving their goals as long as they remain true to themselves. The contrary will be the case for those who are bad. If it absolutely has to be accepted that things turned out differently from what should have occurred, then ways can normally be found to explain that the right outcome has merely been deferred until some future time. Likewise, the apparent triumph of those who are wrong will be purely temporary, since it occurred for reasons which did not reflect any intrinsic virtue in their group or their cause. In this way values can appear to be 'proved' by outcomes appropriate to the validity or invalidity of values and of the people who hold them.

Of course, not all mythopoeic political narratives become established as fully fledged myths. Any given mythopoeic story may or may not come to be accepted as true and authoritative by a particular social group (while being perceived as false or distorted, and hence as 'myth' in the pejorative sense, by another group), even though all mythopoeic discourse contributes cumulatively to the continuous drip-feed of ideological communication in modern societies.

Both Pétain and de Gaulle were mythmakers in the sense defined above. Each sought to narrativise the war and the Occupation in ideologically coloured terms which supported his own political projects and conferred legitimacy on his claims to national leadership. This involved (a) interpreting the present situation in the light of the near or more distant past; and (b) using interpretations of present and past as warrants for predictions of the future – usually conditional predictions linked to exhortations to act or refrain from acting in particular ways so that a positive outcome would be achieved and/or a negative outcome avoided.

As far as the respective ideological marking of Pétain's and de Gaulle's speeches is concerned, the crucial opposition for present purposes can be conveniently summarised in terms of Michel Winock's distinction between closed and open forms of nationalism.[5] Pétain's neo-traditionalist conception of moral, social and political order is linked to the current of reactionary, xenophobic, Right-wing nationalism which starts from an inward-looking preoccupation with decadence, and the need to rectify it through the construction of an authoritarian, corporative regime to make the nation strong once again. De Gaulle's discourse, on the other hand, implicitly appeals to the outward-looking, messianic or liberatory nationalism bequeathed to the republican and the Bonapartist traditions by the new conceptions of citizenship, sovereignty and self-determination enshrined in the culture of the French Revolution. At the same time, the two speakers both underpin their arguments by appeal to a range of general moral values, and each attempts to annex these exclusively to his own interpretation of events.

Mode of Address and Narratorial Posture

The authority of the teller of the story is an essential aspect of mythmaking. To influence the political behaviour of a group by addressing it with words it is necessary for the speaker to claim,

---

5. See M. Winock, *Nationalisme, antisémitisme et fascisme en France*, Paris, Seuil, 1990, pp. 11-40.

and to be granted, legitimacy (right to speak, capacity to give valid interpretations) by addressees. It is a question of symbolic power, as Pierre Bourdieu would say.[6] There needs to be an appropriate fit between the status of the teller and the types of knowledge required to recount a particular story.

Both Pétain and de Gaulle made strategic reference to themselves in order to validate their accounts of events. The Marshal often used himself, in the personal pronoun *je*, as guarantor of the truth of his words. '*Ce n'est pas moi qui vous bernerai par des paroles trompeuses,*' he assures his listeners. '*Je hais les mensonges qui vous ont fait tant de mal*' ('I won't be the one to dupe you with misleading information. I hate the lies that have done you so much harm') (*Discours aux Français*, p. 66, henceforth referred to as *DF*). His projection of his role as leader was not based solely on the formal legitimacy of his official appointment as prime-minister, to which he referred in his first speech. The same speech also contained the famous words about making a gift of himself to France, which he was to echo on a number of occasions throughout the Occupation (see, for example, *DF*, 107, 281). Throughout the War his broadcasts to the nation reinforced appeals to duty with a vocabulary which implied an ineradicable emotional bond between himself and the population. The speeches conveyed a sacrificial, redemptive persona which Gérard Miller rightly describes as a fusion of God the father and Christ the son.[7] They also drew implicitly on the legends surrounding his earlier career, and in particular on his reputation as the patient, compassionate, steadfast commander who had led the French forces at Verdun to endure the onslaught and to do their duty.[8] The plain, unadorned style of his speeches fitted this persona. As he remarked in one of his moralising homilies, '*le langage net et clair est le seul qui puisse se parler. Il ne faut pas se bercer d'illusions, si l'on ne veut pas être victime de désillusions*' ('Clear, unambiguous language is all that can be spoken. We must not be lulled by illusions if we want to avoid becoming victims of disillusionment') (*DF*, 99).

When necessary, the self-referential mode of discourse allowed Pétain to substitute his own authority for real explanation. For example, at the time of the armistice there was no explicit account

---

6. On this aspect, see P. Bourdieu, *Language and Symbolic Power*, trans. G. Raymond and M. Adamson, Cambridge, Polity, 1991.

7. Miller, *Les Pousse-au-jouir*, pp. 51-7.

8. See Pierre Servent, *Le Mythe Pétain : Verdun ou les tranchées de la mémoire*, Paris, Payot, 1992.

of the reasons for not continuing the War from North Africa. Instead, there was Pétain's representation of his honour, as he said: *'Je ne serais pas digne de rester à votre tête si j'avais accepté de répandre le sang des Français pour prolonger le rêve de quelques Français mal instruits des conditions de la lutte'* ('I would not deserve to remain your leader if I had agreed to shed French blood in order to prolong the dream of certain Frenchmen who did not know what was really at stake in the struggle') (*DF*, 65). The force of such claims was buttressed by the fact that the Marshal often cast himself as a quasi-omniscient narrator who voiced what he gave to be the collective thoughts of the French people, in utterances such as *'Elle [la France] a conscience d'avoir mérité le respect du monde'* ('France knows that she has earned the world's respect') (*DF*, 61). This not only allowed him to define motives, hopes and fears in terms which suited his account of events. It also had the symbolic value of reinforcing his claim to leadership. The leader's authority warrants the interpretation, but the act of giving the interpretation underpins the authority of the leader.

Like Pétain, de Gaulle affected a highly personalised form of self-representation at the start, and an assumption of authority in the style of *'croyez-moi, moi qui vous parle en connaissance de cause...'* ('Believe me, I know what I'm talking about') (*Discours et messages*, p. 3, henceforth referred to as *DM*) or *'moi, général de Gaulle, soldat et chef français, j'ai conscience de parler au nom de la France'* ('I, General de Gaulle, French soldier and leader, am conscious that I speak in the name of France')(*DM*, 4). However, whereas frequent use of direct self-reference remained a characteristic feature of Pétain's discourse throughout the War, de Gaulle's own use of it diminished over time. It did so by virtue of his implicit assertion of narratorial omniscience. Like Pétain, de Gaulle purported from the outset to know what the French people were thinking. He knew, for example, that the vast majority of French people rejected the armistice in June 1940 and wanted to continue the war. He could say unhesitatingly of France that *'elle sait, elle sent, qu'elle vaut mieux que la servitude acceptée par le Gouvernement de Bordeaux'* ('She knows, she feels, that she is worth more than the slavery accepted by the Bordeaux government') (*DM*, 6).

This assumption of privileged knowledge of the collective consciousness, or even the soul, of the French nation – and of other historical actors, including the Vichyite authorities, the Germans, or the Allies – allowed de Gaulle to move from the bluster of the early weeks, when verbal self-representation had compensated for his movement's lack of real substance, to the role of prophetic voice delegated to speak for the mind and soul of the true France, as opposed to the hollow replica created by Vichyite discourse and policy. This was what allowed him to construct the myth, according to which the entirety of the French nation, with the exception of a mere handful of Vichyites and Nazi sympathisers, was engaged in resistance of one form or another. Since resistance could be construed simply as a state of mind known to de Gaulle, even those who were doing nothing were part of the national struggle. The underlying supposition was articulated, for example, in a speech to a meeting in London on 1 March 1941: '*Car la France est une, la France est indivisible, et nous savons tous que ce qui se passe dans le coeur des trois mille Français que nous sommes, se passe en même temps dans celui des quarante-deux millions d'autres*' ('France is one and indivisible, and we all know that what touches the hearts of the three thousand Frenchmen here, touches the hearts of forty-two million others at the same time') (*DM*, 69). This enabled him, later in the same speech, to claim that '*dans toutes les villes, tous les bourgs, tous les villages, [la nation française] tisse le réseau secret de sa résistance*' ('In every town, village and hamlet, the French nation is weaving the secret web of resistance') (*DM*, 70).

Conversely, there is an imbalance between the two men's manners of referring to each other. At the outset de Gaulle's speeches made frequent references to the declarations, the policies and the practices of the Vichy government as a whole or of Pétain in particular. He even addressed one of his early speeches directly to the Marshal: '*Monsieur le Maréchal, par les ondes, au-dessus de la mer, c'est un soldat français qui va vous parler*'('Monsieur le Maréchal, over the airwaves, across the sea, a French soldier is going to speak to you') (*DM*, 8). Direct address, soldier to soldier, also implied leader to leader in this context. As Jean Touchard observes, the tone became more bitter and contemptuous after Pétain's announcement of collaboration with Germany in October 1940.[9] Over the course of time de Gaulle's repeated condemnations of Pétain and his government became almost ritualised like a mantra, playing constantly on the theme of betrayal by emphasising the extent of Vichy's dependence on Germany.

Pétain's approach was different. For the first few weeks he did not acknowledge the existence of the upstart general and his motley little force at all. He denied them any legitimacy by ignoring them.

9. See Touchard, *Le Gaullisme*, p. 59.

Subsequently, he still did not refer to de Gaulle by name, and he did not allow the activity of the Free French to intrude often, but merely alluded obliquely and infrequently to them in contemptuous terms such as *'de faux amis qui sont souvent de vrais ennemis'* ('false friends who are often real enemies') (*DF*, 71) or *'la dissidence'* ('dissidents') (*DF*, 121, 140, 325), *'prêcheurs de tumulte'* ('preachers of unrest') (*DF*, 307) or *'terroristes à la solde de l'étranger'* ('terrorists in the pay of foreigners') (*DF*, 313). Nevertheless, the existence of de Gaulle as a voice of opposition was scarcely unknown to Pétain and his entourage from the outset – Pétain signed de Gaulle's death sentence on 2 August 1940. In fact, Pétain often framed his speeches in terms which sought to counter or pre-empt the types of claims articulated by de Gaulle in his BBC radio broadcasts, because de Gaulle voiced objections which could be raised by people within France. In this sense, the two men's representations of what was happening to their country were at least partly interdependent.

Pétain's mythmaking

The entire structure of Pétain's and de Gaulle's wartime mythmaking hinged on their respective interpretations of the meaning of the defeat in 1940. Pétain was Head of State because of the defeat, and de Gaulle was leader of the FFL (*Forces Françaises Libres*, the Free French Forces) for the same reason. Like any historian, the political mythmaker seeks to explain major events in terms of their causes and effects. But the concern of the mythmaker is also to select and interpret information as a source of ideological lessons for the present and future. That means describing causes of unwelcome events in ways which assign blame to adherents of 'wrong' political beliefs, while defending the efforts of the holders of 'right' beliefs to prevent or rectify the damage to society. From the ideological standpoint, especially in extreme situations, it is common to suggest conspiracy, or at least objective collusion, between ideological enemies at home and evil forces abroad. Conspiracy myths help to explain why bad things happen to good people,[10] and they fit the binary *us/them* = *right/wrong* = *good/bad* world of ideological competition. Conversely, the forces

10. See C. Graumann and S. Moscovici (eds), *Changing Conceptions of Conspiracy*, New York, Springer-Verlag, 1987; and for French cases, R. Girardet, *Mythes et mythologies politiques*, Paris, Seuil, 1986, pp. 25-62.

contending to produce the triumph of true beliefs will also tend to be shown as being linked together in their just cause.

The defeat in 1940 lent itself to being represented as a radical historical break. In a sense this suited the Vichyite project, since Pétain's government was there to mitigate the worst consequences of the disaster and, over the longer term, to revive the country as far as circumstances allowed. This presupposed that the causes of the disaster should be identified, that these factors should be prevented from doing further damage, and that their agents should be seen to be punished. Blame for the defeat had to be distributed in such a way as to displace it from the military planners – among whom Pétain himself had played a central role through most of the interwar period – and likewise to exclude the present high command, several of whom were now members of Pétain's government. To explain France's present situation also required dealing with the stark contrast between France's stubborn, and ultimately victorious, resistance to German invasion in 1914-18, in which Pétain had made his own reputation, and the present, humiliating situation in which he had been appointed Prime Minister to negotiate an armistice after a mere few weeks of fighting. The interwar years were the most obvious period in which to locate the sources of this disparity. They fitted conveniently into the schema of decline and fall, with the defeat figuring both as the disastrous culmination of a period of error and as the salutary shock which could precede the slow climb back to greatness if the nation united in submission to Pétain's guidance. Reference to the more distant past would be required as evidence of the permanent, essential qualities of the nation which needed to be restored.

As Hilary Footitt and John Simmonds have pointed out, Pétain's early speeches anticipated the tone and much of the pattern of explanation which he was to develop throughout the war.[11] His primary concern during the second half of June 1940 was to justify the government's course of action, explain its acceptance of the German conditions, and look to the future. The armistice was presented as necessary from the military standpoint by emphasising the catastrophic nature of the situation before the ceasefire. It also had to be honourable in the moral sense. Hence, Pétain made constant play with the gallantry of the French forces in their heroic

11. H. Footitt and J. Simmonds, 'Destroying the Myths of Débâcle, in A.C. Pugh (ed.) *France 1940: Literary and Historical Reactions to Defeat*, Durham, University of Durham, 1991, pp. 19-33.

struggle against overwhelming odds and their willingness to continue doing so, had it not been for the government's reluctant decision. Furthermore, the soldiers' magnificent resistance in face of the onslaught acquitted France of its obligations to Britain, its ally, so honour was also safe in that respect.

There was no denunciation of German aggression or treachery. Besides the obvious constraint on Pétain's freedom of expression with regard to Germany, the claim that the armistice was honourable required that the Germans should not be presented as dishonourable. To make an agreement between sovereign states requires, in principle, that each party be considered honourable enough to keep the agreement. The honour of each party warrants that of the other, and of the agreement itself. Hence, the choice of words to imply precisely that: '*Je me suis adressé cette nuit à l'adversaire pour lui demander s'il est prêt à rechercher avec moi, entre soldats, après la lutte et dans l'honneur, les moyens de mettre un terme aux hostilités*' ('Last night I asked our adversary if, after the battle, as men of honour and fellow-soldiers, he would be prepared to seek with me ways of ending hostilities') (*DF*, 58). The claim that the armistice had been honourable later allowed Pétain to justify collaboration with Germany as being undertaken '*dans l'honneur*' (between 'men of honour') (*DF*, 95). In fact, the word *honneur* and a variety of synonyms or near-synonyms recurred constantly in Pétain's speeches throughout the War to justify his policies.

The location of blame could be used as an additional support for the armistice by implying that France's treaty obligations to Britain had been undermined by Britain's own conduct. This was anticipated in an early speech by the use of a misleading comparison between the number of British divisions sent to France in May 1940, and the much larger number of British soldiers serving in France in May 1917 (*DF*, 59). It was also conveyed by his public rejoinder to Churchill, in which he hinted that British calls for continued resistance by France were motivated solely by concern to protect Britain from the Germans. The implication was that France need no longer consider itself morally bound to Britain. The further suggestion that Britain was attempting to stir division among the French people for its own selfish reasons (*DF*, 62) was to become a recurrent theme in later speeches as Britain was substituted for Germany as the foreign aggressor, often designated simply as '*une puissance étrangère*' ('a foreign power') (*DF*, 286, 287, for example) or '*l'étranger*' ('the foreigner') (*DF*, 167, 203) to accentuate its role as the Other in relation to France.

But there was more blame to be distributed, in terms which addressed the humiliating contrast with 1914-18 but laid the responsibility elsewhere than at the door of the high command. Praise for the self-sacrifice of the soldiers in the early speeches contrasted with Pétain's use of vague, sweeping innuendoes alluding to the moral decline of French society before the War. The immediate causes of the defeat – defined as numerical weakness of the French forces, inadequate armaments and weak allies – were ascribed in the first instance to moral failure, selfish demands and the triumph of pleasure-seeking over self-sacrifice, rather than mere policy errors (*DF*, 60). This not only contributed to placing the military outside the sphere of responsibility for defeat, but it also implied a need to eradicate the causes of moral decay. Conversely, if the armistice could be construed as honourable, it opened positive possibilities for the future, even under the harsh conditions imposed by the Germans, pending a definitive peace at some later date.

In the speech on 20 June 1940 Pétain had also combined an implicit reference to his own record in the First World War with the suggestion that, although the present struggle might be over in a military sense, it would continue in the moral sphere: '*J'ai été avec vous dans les jours glorieux. Chef du gouvernement, je suis et resterai avec vous dans les jours sombres. Soyez à mes côtés. Le combat reste le même*' ('I was with you in your time of glory. As Head of Government, I am and shall remain with you in your time of need. Stay at my side. This is the same battle') (*DF*, 60). In this way, the warrior virtues inherent in France's national identity were merely displaced, rather than negated, by military defeat. This fitted with his claim, even before he began to set out the principles of the *Révolution nationale* from July 1940 onwards, that moral purification would underpin a fundamental political and social transformation, '*un ordre nouveau*' ('a new order') and '*un redressement intellectuel et moral*' ('an intellectual and moral recovery') for the future (*DF*, 66).

His frequent use of the word *épreuve* served him well in relation to the defeat, because it covers the meaning of 'trial', both in the sense of suffering, and of testing, which opens onto religious or metaphysical notions concerning the redemptive nature of suffering when it is willingly accepted as an expiation of past sins, and as a spur to the learning of virtue through mastery of the inner self. This is particularly compatible with the notion of submission to higher authority, discipline, conscientious fulfilment of day-to-day duties and uncomplaining acceptance of privation – values which Pétain preached relentlessly thereafter. The French prisoners of war held by Germany were later to be used as potent symbols of stoical virtue and patient sacrifice on behalf of the nation (*DF*, 209-10, for example).[12]

From July 1940 onwards, Pétain's shift to more direct condemnations of the institutions, policies and practices which had allegedly led to the defeat was inevitably tied to factors for which he could purport to show the remedy. His claim to revive the country through the construction of an authoritarian, corporatist politico-economic system, coupled with a restoration of social unity and traditional moral values, relied heavily on his mythologisation of the interwar years in terms of degeneration. Political and economic liberalism, with its divisive, individualistic and hedonistic values – locked in sterile rivalry with its antithetical outgrowths, Socialism and Communism – could bear the ultimate responsibility for fecklessly dissipating the victory of 1914-18, engaging in provocative, inconsistent policies towards Germany and leading France to blunder into war without adequate preparation or reliable allies. The moral guilt was to be shared by all, as was the requirement for repentant submissiveness. *'Ce régime, pourtant, beaucoup d'entre vous l'aimaient'* ('Yet many of you were fond of that regime'), he reminded the people (*DF*, 86).

Having defined the prewar state of French society in terms of disunity, and having asserted that unity under his authority was the key to national revival, his condemnations of the FFL and the FFI (*Forces Françaises de l'Intérieur*, the overall name given to the Resistance groups within France in the Second World War), and eventually of a range of other groups (such as Freemasons, parliamentarians, civil servants, trades unionists) deemed to be obstructing national renewal, described them frequently in terms which suggested objective collusion in dividing French society and reviving the types of behaviour which had dragged France down before the war. Likewise, their treasonable activities could be represented as serving the interests of external enemies, and notably Britain, the devious *puissance étrangère* (foreign power) (*DF*, 166-67, for example).

When Pétain was talking about the past, he preferred to do so by means of impressionistic descriptions and sweeping generalisations rather than by naming or specifying. He alluded to the

---

12. On the wider use of this theme, see S. Fishman, 'Grand Delusions: The Unintended Consequences of Vichy France's Prisoner-of-War Propaganda', *Journal of Contemporary History* 26 (1991):229-54.

failings of *'l'ancien régime'* ('the previous regime') (*DF*, 86, 166, 270), or to *'les fautes de ceux qui nous ont précédés'* ('the mistakes of those who went before us') (*DF*, 306), for example. But he did not even name the Third Republic, and the only speech in which he named particular politicians of the Republic in connection with the faults of the past was the broadcast on 16 October 1941, announcing preparations for the Riom trials. The general vagueness was convenient. Political communicators know that a broad, impressionistic sweep holds more appeal to a mass audience than detailed analysis does. But it also had the strategic value of softening the edges of the harshest charges, in keeping with the Marshal's constant emphasis on the need for national unity and reconciliation under his authority. According to a major policy speech on 10 October 1940, the *Révolution nationale* was to be something new, not a reactionary return to *'une sorte d'ordre moral'* ('a sort of moral order') or *'une revanche des événements de 1936'* ('revenge for the events of 1936') (*DF*, 88). Notwithstanding the Maurrassian inspiration of the *Révolution nationale* or the reality of Vichy's governance, that was Pétain's public posture. Similarly, he did not explicitly repeat the attacks on the heritage of the French Revolution which were characteristic of the reactionary Right. The attitude could merely be inferred from a scattering of indirect comments, the most obvious of which was a set of remarks on the political instability which had haunted France *'depuis cent cinquante ans'* ('for the past 150 years') (*DF*, 148).

Pétain's references to more distant history tended to be equally imprecise and relatively infrequent. He was more inclined to focus on the short term. He would sum up some particular aspect of France's situation since the defeat, acknowledge its painful nature and express his solidarity with the people, explain what needed to be done in order to make the best of that situation, then exhort the audience to do it. Alternatively, he was at home with timeless, general principles, formulated as eternal truths of the type: *'Mais le vrai patriotisme ne saurait s'exprimer que par une fidélité totale. On ne compose ni avec son devoir ni avec sa parole'* ('But true patriotism can only be expressed by total fidelity. One does not compromise with one's duty or one's word of honour') (*DF*, 325). The fundamental suppositions of the *Révolution nationale* itself were given to be permanently valid, not derived from the example of a particular régime. That was why Pétain could still tell the members of the LVF (*Légion des Volontaires Français contre le Bolchevisme*, 'Legion of French Volunteers against Bolchevism'), on 14 August 1944 that even if events had impeded the application of the principles, they could not alter their validity (*DF*, 339).

This is not to say that the Marshal never used the longer-term past as a source of validation and example for the present. In fact, the whole weight of French history (presumably excluding the last 150 years) was supposedly on his side. Characteristically sweeping formulations were of the type: '*Donnons-nous à la France. Elle a toujours porté son peuple à la grandeur*' ('Let us give ourselves to France. She has always borne her people to greatness') (*DF*, 71). Or '*Le peuple français porte son avenir en lui-même, dans la profondeur des soixante générations qui vous ont précédés sur notre sol et dont vous êtes les héritiers responsables*' ('The French people carry their future within them in the sixty generations that preceded you on our land, and as their descendants you bear that responsibility') (*DF*, 155). France was thus being called upon to recognise the facets of its true historical identity, which had been obscured in recent times. That was the underlying meaning in November 1940, when Pétain hailed the progress made up to then with the tautology: '*Vous avez compris qu'aujourd'hui la France est la France*' ('You have understood that today France is France') (*DF*, 98). Specific references to major historical figures as exemplars in Pétain's speeches were particularly rare. Among the monarchs, only Henri IV receives a mention by name when he is cited alongside Jeanne d'Arc, Richelieu and the Convention as a defender of the principles of unity and authority (*DF*, 120). Henri's minister, Sully, is mentioned twice, very briefly (*DF*, 151, 214).

Only Jeanne d'Arc received more substantial treatment, in keeping with her status as a patriotic icon of the régime. This was not an entirely straightforward matter, however, because she could easily be taken as a reproach to Vichy's submissive, collaborative stance towards Germany, given her role in military resistance against a foreign occupying power. On her memorial day in 1941 Pétain gave a very short, insipid speech, hailing the peasant girl as a martyr to national unity and a model of fidelity to the land, to the king and to God. Although Pétain listed '*la délivrance d'Orléans, la chevauchée de Champagne*' ('the deliverance of Orleans, the ride through Champagne') (*DF*, 131) among the stages of her trajectory, he naturally refrained from any call for emulation of that aspect of her activity. The following year the message was much longer. Consequently it was more tortuous and (deliberately or accidentally) ambiguous. Jeanne was again offered as a model of faith, love, self-sacrifice for others, faith in king, country and God, courage and determination in overcoming obstacles. Pétain remarked that she had made the people realise they should unite around their leaders and close their ears to foreign propaganda, just as the nation should do now in order to re-embark on what the Marshal called *'le chemin de ses destinées éternelles'* ('the path of its eternal destiny') (*DF*, 256). Although there was no direct call to follow Jeanne's example of armed resistance to the occupying power, the speech could almost have been taken as a coded message to that effect, had it not been for the fact that Pétain named England as the foreign power whose propaganda had stirred division in Jeanne's time and as the country which let France down in 1940. The tone of the speech was therefore characteristically anti-British, not anti-German.

The problem of citing Jeanne d'Arc may point to one of the reasons for the relative rarity of historical reference in the corpus of speeches. Pétain was not well placed to dwell on France's history as a warrant for his present policies, except in very general terms. The glories of French popular history were associated with the great eras of power and expansion, or else with heroism in the face of adversity, not with acquiescence in defeat and loss of independence. Although the purification and renewal of French society through the medium of the *Révolution nationale* could be presented on a quasi-religious model of sin-expiation-redemption as a form of struggle to overcome inner decay, the emergence of the Resistance and the rise of public dissatisfaction with the privations of the Occupation showed that this appeal had its limits. And the fact remained that the great leaders celebrated in the history books were not those who retained their power by making themselves acceptable to the victorious enemy.

In a similar way, the longer-term future was shrouded in imprecision. Beyond the endlessly reiterated claims that France would revive if the principles of the *Révolution nationale* were fully enacted by the people, it was not specified how this revival would be translated into a place in the geopolitics of the postwar era. Besides the fact that the circumstances of the war and of the Occupation made the future extremely uncertain, Pétain was not free to speculate publicly in the light of any possible outcome other than German victory. This meant that the nation's future could be framed only in terms which were compatible with the presumption that France would take a subordinate place in Germany's New European Order, though a suitable vagueness characterised these references as well. The allusion to France's future role *'dans le cadre d'une activité constructive du nouvel ordre européen'* ('within the framework of the construction of the new European order') (*DF*, 95), made in the speech of 30 October 1940 announcing Franco-German collaboration, was relatively explicit. Later comments were even more cautiously formulated in terms of anticipation of *'une Europe réconciliée'* ('European reconciliation') (*DF*, 205, 222) or words to that effect, coupled on occasion with expressions of gratitude to Germany for leading the crusade against bolshevism (*DF*, 205, 326).

De Gaulle's Mythmaking

The story produced by de Gaulle's speeches during the war was antithetical to Pétain's in many respects, but largely symmetrical in structure. Having made a primary judgement that France's defeat was provisional, not final, and that Germany was not certain to win the War, de Gaulle's objective at the outset had been to deny the validity of the armistice, both in military and in moral terms, while giving reasons for continuing the fight. Like Pétain, he did not blame the ordinary soldiers, but unlike Pétain, he did not blame Britain either, nor did he reproach the civilian population for moral laxity in the past. This allowed him to concentrate responsibility on the high command and Pétain's government, as well as on Germany and Italy, while he implicitly cast himself as defender of the French people and of Britain, the ally deserted by the makers of the armistice.

De Gaulle's use of the past was symmetrical with Pétain's insofar as he too made use of the interwar years in particular as a period of decay which produced the conditions for France's defeat. Like Pétain, he wanted to assert that the fruits and the lessons of France's heroic struggle in 1914-18 had been thrown away. In the early months of the Occupation one of his main concerns was to present the interwar decades as the period when the present leaders of the Vichy régime had been in charge of France's military planning and arms procurement policies. The principal failure on the French side was theirs. If the high command were held guilty of leaving France inadequately armed, and with outdated tactics, and if the government contained members of the high command, led by the man who had dominated defence policy through most of the interwar period, then the government and high command could be identified together in terms of flawed judgement and betrayal of duty. They had betrayed the soldiers who depended on them. They had betrayed the alliance with Britain. They had given way to panic and defeatism. Therefore, by extension, who could trust their claim that the armistice was necessary or honourable? The message was already implicit in the first two sentences of the famous appeal on 18 June: '*Les chefs qui, depuis de nombreuses années, sont à la tête des armées françaises, ont formé un gouvernement. Ce gouvernement, alléguant la défaite de nos armées, s'est mis en rapport avec l'ennemi pour cesser le combat*' ('The leaders who have been at the head of the French forces for many years, formed a government. This government, alleging the defeat of our forces, entered into negotiations with the enemy to end the fighting') (*DM*, 3). In subsequent speeches, such as his broadcast on 24 June, the message was more explicit: '*la France et les Français sont, pieds et poings liés, livrés à l'ennemi*' ('France and the French, bound hand and foot, have been delivered to the enemy') (*DM*, 7). At the same time, by seeking to discredit the competence and the integrity of these people, de Gaulle implicitly defended himself against the charge that he had deserted his own post, disobeyed orders, and further dishonoured himself by fleeing to exile on the territory of Britain, the treacherous ex-ally.

The victorious struggle against Germany in the First World War could therefore serve as a source of contrasts to attack the military men at Vichy, and above all to denigrate Pétain himself. In the wake of the Marshal's broadcast justifying the armistice, de Gaulle's tactic of addressing his own response directly to Pétain produced some impressive rhetoric which included the sentences, mixing anger, contempt and pity: '*La Patrie, le Gouvernement, vous-même, réduits à la servitude. Ah! pour obtenir et pour accepter un pareil acte d'asservissement, on n'avait pas besoin de vous, Monsieur le Maréchal, on n'avait pas besoin du vainqueur de Verdun; n'importe qui aurait suffi*' ('Our country, our Government, you yourself, reduced to slavery. To obtain and accept such an act of enslavement, we did not need you, Marshal Pétain, we did not need the victor of Verdun; anyone would have done') (*DM*, 9). Later in the war, de Gaulle's gambit of using the nickname '*Père-la-défaite*' ('Father Defeat') for Pétain as a parody on Clemenceau's nickname, '*Père-la-victoire*', ('Father Victory') was an aspect of this same exploitation of the irony of Pétain's present situation in the light of his past (*DM*, 123, 205, 229, for example; and 131 for Clemenceau).

Thus, de Gaulle argued that the contrast between 1914-18 and 1940 showed the failure of the military system, not the moral decay of French society as a whole. Pétain's attempt to persuade the civilian population that the defeat was their fault was depicted by de Gaulle as an attempt to crush French morale in the interests of Vichy and the Germans, hence as evidence of objective collusion between the government and the occupying power. In de Gaulle's construction, the First World War had shown the true France, whereas the failings of the interwar years were transitory and superficial, not signs of deeper moral and social decadence.

In the early part of the Occupation de Gaulle showed no inclination to dwell on the political failings of the interwar period of the Third Republic, and thereby risk a loss of differentiation in relation to Pétain. By mid-1942, having endlessly denounced the hollow authoritarianism of the *Révolution nationale*, he was also increasingly willing to allude to the political defects of the prewar Republic in terms which sometimes coincided with those used by Pétain (*DM*, 238-39, 312-13, for example). But by then he was in a position to sketch out the broad lines of the new political and social order which should be set in place after the Liberation and this was defined in terms which distanced it from the characteristics of the Vichy régime by aligning it with the republican tradition.

It was obviously important to counter Vichyite efforts to deflect hostility from the Germans to the British. In opposition to Pétain's account, de Gaulle asserted that France had been right to enter the conflict with Germany, and that this had been a sign of national honour (*DM*, 73), not of incoherent policy, as Pétain claimed. By late 1941 de Gaulle had adopted the gambit of referring to the entire period since 1914 as '*la guerre de trente ans*' ('the Thirty Years War') (*DM*, 136, 139, 198, for example, prefigured by 110). This enabled him to convey the impression that the interwar years had merely been a pause for regrouping between battles as Germany pursued its aggression. Besides reducing the scale of the defeat in 1940 in comparison with the extended duration of the conflict, the device made the military inadequacies of French strategic planning and arms procurement by the high command since 1918 appear all the more serious, the persistence of German aggression all the more vicious, and the present collaboration of Vichy with Germany all the more debased.

Whereas for Pétain, France's rebirth had to come through a transmutation of the arena of struggle from the military sphere to the inner realm of national consciousness through moral and social renewal, de Gaulle treated the armistice conditions as tantamount to enslavement: *asservissement, servitude*, 'enslavement', 'slavery' are the words which recur at the opposite moral pole to the word, *honneur*, which figures in de Gaulle's discourse even more often than in Pétain's. For de Gaulle, in the early stages of the war, it was not so much a case of defining national renewal in terms of moral, social or political change within France. The War itself was represented as the process of renewal, because it was a trial to be undergone with honour, and hence a form of action which called for the highest moral qualities in the service of liberty. Against Vichy's divisive parody of unity under the police state, he offered a dynamic conception of national unity as being forged *'dans la lutte, dans la fierté, dans la victoire'* ('in struggle, pride and victory') (*DM*, 201).

In this context, there was constant emphasis on Free France's solidarity with Britain and the U.S. (whose entry into the war was predicted with certainty from the start, thanks to de Gaulle's narratorial omniscience), as well as with the territories of the French Empire. In contrast to his invective against Hitler and Mussolini, he hymned the praises of Churchill and Roosevelt. He could hardly have done otherwise, given his situation. Nevertheless, his stance was significant, because it expressed a different form of nationalism from Pétain's. The overwhelming emphasis in Pétain's speeches was on the nation withdrawing into itself to find unity. Notwithstanding a few pious references to the future reconciliation of Europe, the war-torn world outside France is a source of threat and aggression to France. For his part, de Gaulle portrayed the fulfilment of national unity as being dependent on participation in a great movement of liberation which potentially extended to the whole world. As the war continued and de Gaulle began to expound on the future postwar order, his model for French government and society as free, democratic, and socio-economically inclusive was habitually framed within the wider context of the new, free, democratic, international order (e.g., *DM*, 109-11, 201-4). The emphasis on inclusiveness in these spheres paralleled de Gaulle's conception of the wartime Resistance movement in which almost everyone was deemed to be playing a valuable part, if only by tacit solidarity.

Unlike Pétain, de Gaulle was free to deploy all the uplifting glories of French history over the centuries in support of his cause. This could be done either negatively to attack Pétain and his government, or positively to add weight to his representation of Free France. For example, Crécy and Sedan could be cited as historical precedents for defeat caused by inadequate military strategy and armaments, not by a general failure of the nation (*DM*, 72). France's great political and military figures of the past could be cited as exemplars and precursors for the struggle to win the victory. The builders of the empire could be called in support of the fight to liberate the colonies. Much quoted though it has been, it is worth recalling the speech on 2 July 1940 in which he summoned up a succession of these names as testimony on behalf of his claim that France's soul was with those who fight on to victory:

> *Jeanne d'Arc, Richelieu, Louis XIV, Carnot, Napoléon, Gambetta, Poincaré, Clemenceau, le Maréchal Foch, auraient-ils jamais consenti à livrer toutes les armes de la France à ses ennemis pour qu'ils puissent s'en servir contre ses Alliés? Duquesne, Tourville, Suffren, Courbet, Guépratte, auraient-ils jamais consenti émettre à la discrétion de l'ennemi une flotte française intacte?*

> *Dupleix, Montcalm, Bugeaud, le maréchal Lyautey, auraient-ils jamais consenti à évacuer, sans combattre, les points stratégiques de l'Empire, auraient-ils jamais supporté, sans même avoir livré combat, le contrôle de l'ennemi sur l'Empire?*

(Would Joan of Arc, Richelieu, Louis XIV, Carnot, Napoleon, Gambetta, Poincaré, Clemenceau, or Marshal Foch ever have consented to deliver up France's entire stock of weapons to their enemies, so that they could be used against her allies? Would Duquesne, Tourville, Suffren, Courbet or Guépratte ever have consented to put a French fleet, whole and entire, at the enemy's disposal? Would Dupleix, Montcalm, Bugeaud, or Marshal Lyautey ever have consented to abandon the strategic points of the Empire without a fight, would they ever have accepted enemy control of the Empire without even giving battle?) (*DM*, 12)

As her inclusion in the list quoted above suggests, Jeanne d'Arc could be a symbol in de Gaulle's discourse, not only of patriotism, fidelity, self-sacrifice and other values cited by Pétain, but also of armed resistance to the occupier and to the traitors who collaborated (*DM*, 85, 111, 183) – the fact that the occupier in Jeanne's day had been Britain was not something on which de Gaulle chose to dwell. By the end of the war, de Gaulle also had the heroes of the FFL itself to cite in similarly epic vein, as he recalled '*cette équipe des Catroux, des Larminat, des Eboué, des Koenig, des Leclerc, des Pleven, des d'Argenlieu, des Cassin, des Boislambert, autour de laquelle se serrèrent, au lendemain du désastre, les hommes qui ne renonçaient pas*' ('the team of Catroux, Larminats, Eboués, Koenigs, Leclercs, Plevens, d'Argenlieus, Cassins, Boislamberts, around whom clustered the men who refused to give up in the wake of disaster') (*DM*, 376).

De Gaulle's use of historical reference was also more extensive and expansive than Pétain's in relation to political principles for the future ordering of French society. Although Pétain claimed that the *Révolution nationale* was a harmonious synthesis between authority and liberties, with the implication that, as its very name suggested, it bridged the divide between the opposing currents of the period since 1789, the reality was that its principles, as well as its practice, leaned far more heavily to the authoritarian and traditionalist side. During the Occupation, de Gaulle's model for the future was not put to the test of practice except in the establishment of provisional institutions. However, its discursive construction could benefit from his willingness to include references incorporating both pre- and post-Revolution history in a unified, though selective sweep which was presented as leading inevitably to the rebirth of the country after the achievement of victory, because the very essence of the French nation was to create and recreate itself over the centuries as a cohesive entity. To quote one striking example from a speech on 6 June 1943:

> *Du plus profond de notre peuple s'est élevé cet instinct vital qui, depuis bientôt deux mille ans, nous a maintes fois tirés des abîmes. C'est cet instinct qui fit chrétiens les Francs et les Gaulois de Clovis, quand sur les ruines de leur paganisme se précipitaient les Barbares. C'est cet instinct qui suscita Jeanne d'Arc et entraîna les Français à bâtir, autour du roi, un Etat centralisé, lorsqu'il parut que l'anarchie féodale nous livrait à la domination étrangère. C'est cet instinct qui, lors de la Révolution, dressa la nation contre ses ennemis et contre leurs complices et lui dicta, pour la sauver, les grands principes des Droits de l'Homme et de la Démocratie. C'est cet instinct qui, aujourd'hui, porte tous les Français soucieux de l'avenir et de la grandeur de la patrie à vouloir et à préparer la Quatrième République: celle de la rénovation nationale.*

(From the depths of our nation has risen the vital instinct that for nearly 2000 years has so often saved us from the abyss. This was the instinct that turned Clovis's Franks and Gauls to Christianity, when barbarians flung themselves onto the ruins of their pagan society. This was the instinct which stirred Joan of Arc and led Frenchmen to build a centralised state around the king when it seemed that feudal anarchy was delivering us up to domination by a foreign power. This was the instinct which made the nation stand up against its enemies and their accomplices at the time of the Revolution, and dictated the great principles of the Rights of Man and Democracy, to save it. This is the instinct which today leads all Frenchmen concerned for the future of their country and her greatness, to desire and prepare for the Fourth Republic, bringing national renewal.) (*DM*, 300)

This perspective equally linked France to a pivotal place in the future international order. For example, while the makers of the Empire could be named in evidence of France's civilising mission as an imperial power (*DM*, 371), the transmission of the principles of the Revolution warranted the claim to solidarity with the U.S. on the basis of its own Revolution. In short, France was permanently destined to play a vital role among the nations because it was bound to them, as he put it on 1 March 1941, by virtue of '*un pacte vingt fois séculaire entre la grandeur de la France et la liberté du monde*' ('a pact made twenty centuries ago between the greatness of France and the freedom of the world.') (*DM*, 73)

Conclusion

Pétain and de Gaulle produced radically different accounts of the meaning of the defeat, the armistice and the Occupation. However, the underlying framework of interpretation was the same in each case. In the course of their speeches both Pétain and de Gaulle used the assumption of narratorial omniscience to represent France's situation in terms which presupposed a form of ideological essentialism, a characteristic feature of political mythmaking. That is to say, each assumed that he knew the fundamental nature, the trans-historical essence, of the French nation. When referring to France in his speeches, each could therefore distinguish what was essential and permanent from what was merely incidental, or at least changeable, in its nature. He could discern its fundamental needs. Because both men purported to know France in this way, they could grasp the meaning of its past to interpret what was happening in the present and to anticipate the future. Ideological essentialism does not entail thoroughgoing determinism, otherwise there could be no freedom, no self-determination and hence no moral value. But, as in de Gaulle's and Pétain's discourse, it lends itself to conditional forms of prediction in which a set of possible outcomes is framed in the light of what is appropriate to the actor's nature, given the range of possible actions permitted by an anticipated historical context. The story could then serve as a warrant for an injunction to think and act in ways which would achieve the right outcome. Each of the two men told a story of decline and fall, a story of betrayal, a story of salvation through struggle and sacrifice, a story of national rebirth, and a story of the redemptive leader who guides the nation towards unity in renewal. These are the classic scenarios of mythmaking. The two men's stories explain the meaning of how things are now, and how they came to be that way. They distinguish the agents of good from the agents of evil. They offer guarantees of future rewards for those who follow the right course of action as prescribed by the speaker. And paradoxically, as is often the case in situations of conflict, they talk indirectly to each other, so that their antagonistic interdependence leads them to contribute to the construction of each other's stories.

6

BETWEEN PROPAGANDA AND TELLING THE TRUTH

The Underground French Press during
The Occupation (1940-1944)

Olivier Wieviorka

It is as well to stress from the outset that the underground press and the high-circulation democratic press operated in radically different registers. In peacetime, as is well known, the main aim of newspapers is to convince and/or inform. Underground periodicals, on the other hand, assumed very different functions. They sought, of course, to spread information. However, this ambition received support from some very unlikely quarters, and the Resistance was sometimes forced to decide between contradictory options. Thus the strict control exercised by the Vichy régime and the Occupation authorities was an invitation to defy censorship and encouraged the underground press to use the language of truth. From this point of view 'the shadow army' (to take up the image suggested in 1943 by Joseph Kessel in the novel of the same name) raised up against the lies of State systems the debilitating responsibility of speaking the truth. A vast programme indeed. The German authorities and their Vichy allies did not hesitate to lie by deliberately distorting a reality which they knew to be true (for example, denying the defeats in Russia). They also created myths by offering partial or idealised portrayals showing the invincibility of the Wehrmacht, and the French community united around Marshal Pétain. These facts might lead the Resistance members to give the raw facts – a high-risk gamble. It assumed that the public, judged *a priori* to be mature, was ready to hear distressing truths (for example, the rapid advance of the German armies into Russia, the fall of Singapore, etc.) and that hearing bad news would shake neither their morale, nor their resolve – two dimensions which were obviously crucial to achieve victory. On the other hand, as can be imagined, the underground press could, by being economical with the truth, resort to propaganda on their own account. Spreading information painted in the colours of hope – minimising Allied defeats, exaggerating the slightest victory, denying the real popularity of Marshal Pétain and the solidity of the Nazi régime – could then contribute to supporting the morale of a population depressed by the strange defeat, worn out by the Occupation, driven to despair by the invincibility of the Wehrmacht. This approach would also allow them to set up, against the verbal excesses of Vichy or the Nazis, a counterattack of language couched in the same terms, addressing imagination rather than cold reason. By opening up a space to dream, this strategy could finally enable the Resistance to obtain both the support and the involvement of the civilian population since, if Chateaubriand is to be believed, a nation, be it French or otherwise, is only held together if it is led onwards by dreams. The Resistance thus confronted a cruel dilemma. To demythologise Vichy and Nazi words forced it to tell the truth – and thus guarantee its own credibility, since it then legitimised itself by revealing the lies and myths of the enemy. The BBC's unhesitating announcement of bad news, played a great part in capturing its audience. Listeners were convinced that the English airwaves always spoke the language of truth. However, to raise the morale of civilians, to rally and mobilise them, the weapon of truth was sometimes a very mediocre resource, and propaganda a strong temptation. Could they hope to mobilise the French by parading Allied defeats, by stressing the solidity of the Nazi régime, by insisting on the exceptionally small minority who supported the Resistance, and its weak resources? Certainly not! Therefore it can be easily understood how the underground press was divided between two contradictory necessities (to tell the truth, to distort the facts) without, however, wanting or being able to cut this Gordian knot. Certainly the diversity of the underground press forces us to reject any generalisation. However the tightness of constraints (for example, censorship, repression, etc.), the similarity of objectives (to mobilise the population against the occupier, etc.), the similarity of choices (on the language to adopt, the strategy to follow, etc.), compelled them in general to face up to comparable problems and accept similar solutions.

Taking this as read, an analysis of the underground press would tend to be rather reassuring, as newspapers favoured truth (i.e., the honest reporting of the facts) rather than lies (the deliberate wish to transform them). Military information, in particular, challenged any extravagant language – even if it meant driving the readership to despair. For example, 'We would not think (…) of hiding the defeats suffered during these last few weeks in our Allied campaigns,'[1] noted *Combat*, a newspaper from the Southern Zone, parading a litany of depressing news, in particular the fall of Singapore. On 1 March 1942, *Libération-sud* – a Southern periodical which is readily classified as being left-wing – admitted that 'the Japanese attack, although it had been expected for a long time, was infinitely more brutal and more powerful than the Allies expected (…). It cannot even be ruled out that the war in the east may be a long one, and continue for many months after hostilities have ended in Europe'.[2] And far from showing blind optimism, *Les Petites Ailes*, the paper of a moderate movement in northern France, asserted in 1941 that the Reich, in the Soviet Union, 'will obtain initial successes. Will they be lasting? Only the future will tell because Russia is in a position to wage a long war and other factors may weigh heavily in the balance'.[3]

Certainly, the underground newspapers did not hesitate, sometimes, to distort reality, deliberately twisting it. 'In one week, Hitler has lost 1,500 aeroplanes, 2,500 tanks and 30,000 prisoners' proclaimed *L'Humanité*, which, on 1 July 1941, was surprising.[4] The Communist publication[5] went even further: 'The Red Army has put nine million Nazis out of the war, of whom four million have been killed', an astonishing toll, to say the least. Likewise, the underground press sometimes repeated fanciful information. 'It is thought that Hitler is seriously ill' asserted *Résistance*, a newspaper appearing in the Northern Zone. 'It is for that reason that newspapers, by order, have recently been publishing photographs of the Führer on the Russian front, but reading Ordnance Survey maps, and these photos appear to be old'[6]. And *Défense de la France*,

---

1. *Combat*, 2 February 1942.
2. 'Echecs passagers, certitudes croissantes', *Libération*, 1 March 1942.
3. *Les Petites Ailes*, 1 July 1941.
4. *L'Humanité*, 2 July 1941.
5. 'Le salut est dans le combat', *L'Humanité*, 1 April 1943.
6. *Résistance*, no. 3, August 1941.

a publication from the Northern Zone, picking up 'the state of disintegration in which Germany finds itself' asserted that popular support for Hitler's régime was crumbling[7] – a remarkably optimistic view when it is known that the German population was to retain its confidence in the Führer until 1944, to the extent of disapproving of the assassination attempt carried out on 20 July 1944!

The extent to which these false rumours were believed, however, remained limited. Beyond the desire to raise public morale, the publication of such lies reflected above all the importance of rumour, a common phenomenon in wartime, and proved, on the contrary, the despair of a Resistance reduced to hoping for victory by a miracle (Hitler's illness, in this case). However, on the whole, the underground press refrained from any triumphalism in the military domain. Moreover, to avoid any drift towards propaganda, it did not hesitate to quote the foreign media. *Défense de la France*, for example, referred to the *Journal de Genève*,[8] the BBC,[9] and even the German press,[10] an elegant way of demonstrating its own impartiality.

By using an informative register – where the raw fact is reported without comment – the underground press sought to undermine the influence of enemy propaganda. The desire to counter the prevailing language thus led the Resistance to favour two methods of contribution. It endeavoured, first of all, to bring to the attention of the public facts carefully hidden by censorship. Besides the military failures which they reported with great delight, the newspapers denounced the crimes of the occupiers and their Vichy allies. *Franc-Tireur* as well as *Combat* revealed the militia's involvement in the assassination of Maurice Sarraut, which Vichy shamelessly attributed to the Resistance.[11] *Défense de la France* revealed the atrocities that the Germans or the French police were committing in prisons and in concentration camps.[12] However, the Resistance also sometimes adopted an interpretative approach. Even when not actually revealing facts hidden by censorship, it interpreted events known to all in order to construct a

7. Pelletier (Alphonse Dain), 'Un tract allemand', *Défense de la France*, no. 19, July 1942.

8. 'Stratégie mondiale', article taken from the *Journal de Genève*, 31 December 1941, quoted in *Défense de la France*, no. 7, 1 January 1942.

9. 'Dernière minute', *Défense de la France*, no. 9, 25 January 1942.

10. 'Le soldat russe', taken from *Schwarze Korps* (newspaper of the SS), *Défense de la France*, no. 28, 20 February 1943

11. 'Les Miliciens ont tué Sarraut', *Franc-Tireur*, 6 May 1944; 'Les assassins de Sarraut sont connus', *Combat*, December 1943.

12. 'Les fruits de la haine', *Défense de la France*, no. 39, 30 September 1943.

meaning contradicting interpretations placed on them by the enemy. *Combat* recalled for example the fact that contrary to what the official press was asserting 'the English have undertaken never to steal our Empire from us'.[13] *L'Humanité* stressed that because of their responsibility for the French army's unprepared state, 'Pétain and Darlan ought to be among the main defendants at the Riom trial'.[14] *Franc-Tireur* asserted that the fall of Mussolini could be called an 'impressive and striking return to justice'.[15] All the newspapers, finally, defended the Allied bombing raids,[16] which the French population found difficult to tolerate, a feeling immediately exploited by Vichy and the Germans. By developing counterpropaganda, the Resistance placed itself therefore deliberately on the same ground as the enemy, turning its reasoning around. However, whether resorting to information or interpretation, it addressed the French people's reason first and foremost, eschewing any appeal to feelings or emotions.

By adopting this approach, the Resistance was clearly distancing itself from the methods adopted during the First World War since it rejected brainwashing which had, in the end, been counterproductive. This strategy was also aimed at keeping the French in the fight. Misplaced optimism might have legitimised the wait-and-see policy and pushed the French to exonerate themselves from the need to fight. 'Let us keep a close watch on our imagination, pleasant precursor of a success still to come. And let us not lose sight of the fact that the German is there, still there. He will not run away, one fine morning, without any bloodshed. In order to chase him out hard battles will be necessary, in which Frenchmen not in uniform will have their own military role. If we are tempted to lose sight of the main objective by eager anticipation of a better future, we must resolutely suppress such longings,' warned *Résistance*,[17] for example, here eager for realism.

This need for truth should not be treated as mere opportunism, aiming both to keep the French in the War and to challenge the dubious legacy of the Great War. By refusing to manipulate its readership, the underground press remained faithful to its ethics.

13. 'Vous l'avait-on dit', *Combat*, 1 September 1943.

14. 'Le procès de Riom', *L'Humanité*, 9 March 1942.

15. 'Mussolini s'effondre, et d'un!', *Franc-Tireur*, 25 July 1943.

16. 'Le bombardement des usines Renault', *L'Humanité*, 9 March 1942; 'A propos des raids alliés', *Franc-Tireur*, 6 May 1944.

17. Joseph Ricou, 'D'abord, nous faisons la guerre', *Résistance*, no. 19, 20 November 1943.

As commitment to the Resistance was based on a free and voluntary act, the Resistance movements wanted to convince and not to indoctrinate. They therefore sought to help their fellow citizens form a judgement so that they would commit themselves in full possession of the facts. This dimension was explicitly perceived and taken on board by the underground press. By clearly defining what was at stake in the conflict, 'every Frenchman will be able to choose: he will be for us or against us' explained *Combat*.[18] 'This bearing of Christian witness will speak of the unavoidable urgency to form a single battle front which commits us all jointly in the brotherly communion of a truth stronger than the contagion of lies which are only triumphant for a short while,' asserted for its part the periodical of Father de Montcheuil.[19] One implicit principle underpins this reasoning: truth will always come out in the end, which enabled *Combat* to consider it as a 'weapon'.[20] For 'while the lie, printed in millions of copies, retains a certain power, it is sufficient that the truth be told for the lie to retreat'.[21]

This approach was founded on an observation: the defeat of 1940 as well as the popular support for the Vichy regime followed on, in part, from the lies with which the French had been swamped. However, by asserting the pre-eminence of truth, the Resistance movements were also, and perhaps above all, following a double tradition. They supported a positivist republican model, heir of the Enlightenment, which insisted on educating citizens and whose morality denounced hypocrites and liars. In spite of his Marxist beliefs, even someone like Jaurès supported this idea since he believed that Socialism would prevail thanks largely to the education of the masses. The French Resistance was also inspired by a Christian legacy which compared the victory of Christ to the triumph of truth. For obvious reasons, this link was explicitly stated by *Témoignage chrétien*: 'By bearing witness against anti-Semitism for truth and justice, we are bearing witness for Christ'. Numerous movements subscribed to this approach. *Défense de la France*, for example, placed in its headline the famous saying of Pascal: 'I believe only those histories whose witnesses are willing to be butchered' (*Pensées*, no. 397). On the other hand, political groups operating in a traditional military way, political parties above all, did not share such a belief. *L'Humanité* illus-

18. 'Appel', *Combat*, no. 1, December 1941.
19. '2ème Cahier' du *Témoignage chrétien*, December 1941.
20. 'Appel', *Combat*, no. 1, December 1941.
21. 'A guerre totale, résistance totale', *Combat*, March 1944.

trated this prejudice to the point of caricature. Not hesitating to reproduce falsehood after falsehood, and favouring the indoctrination of individuals in their education, the French Communist Party ostensibly differed from tendencies retained by the Resistance movements anxious, as has been seen, to give information which, while not being objective, was at least honest. The Resistance counted on the maturity of the French, believing that a speech, even bearing disastrous news, would be heard by responsible and reasonable public opinion.

This gamble did not prevent the Resistance movements from displaying certain fears with regard to the civilian population. The relationship which the Resistance maintained with the civilian population was an ambivalent one. Thus the population, whose patriotism was applauded, was sometimes presented as an ally of the Resistance. 'In spite of the commotion made by propaganda, in spite of the intimidating nature of power, in spite of the desertion of the ruling classes, the people of our country, all parties and all milieux together, see the truth and recognise their duty,' noted *Combat*, for example, in July 1942.[22] '999 French out of 1,000 wish and want Hitler to be defeated. Thus our country, hitherto so divided, is finding its unity again,' *L'Humanité* noted in July 1941.[23] Conversely, the French were sometimes blamed, either because they were judged jointly responsible for a defeat from which they could not be exonerated, or because their wait-and-see policy and their spinelessness were denounced. 'How can it be that there are still some French who stand aside from the struggle? What are these long queues in front of cinemas, long queues of poor human beings who have come to seek their ration of pleasure, poor beings without any other aspiration than a full stomach? Who are those young people, studious, moderate, calm, passive, well-behaved, reasonable, when the sound of battle has not yet died away in Africa?.... French men and women, when will you understand that we are at war, and that war is more than just listening to English radio!' exclaimed *Défense de la France* in 1943.[24] The underground press thus worked with conflicting portrayals, presenting the French sometimes as victims, sometimes as accomplices of the occupier, two visions which were obviously irreconcilable. To rally a population whose wait-and-see policy was denounced, the

22. *Combat*, July 1942.

23. 'Françaises! Français! vous devez savoir que Hitler veut asservir tous les peuples', *L'Humanité*, special edn, July 1941.

24. 'La France est en guerre', *Défense de la France*, no. 33, 20 May 1943.

underground press then left the domain of information or interpretation in order to venture onto other shores.

The Resistance endeavoured to arouse the exasperation of the
French by counting on tested patriotic motives and by banking on
the material difficulties of the population.

The underground press thus devoted page after page to Alsace-
Lorraine. Besides the Germanisation of the lost provinces, *Défense
de la France* denounced the Nazi terror which manifested itself by
pressing young people into service, and the massive deportations
and internment in concentration camps.[25] These descriptions corresponded with reality – although they underestimated the Germanophobia of a not inconsiderable part of the population. 'It is
no lie to say that Alsace sent all its sons without exception to
defend the frontiers of France in 1939. Alsace has continually
resisted the invader for two years,' asserted, for example, *Franc-
Tireur*,[26] whose optimistic conclusions are open to question. Two
thirds of Alsace-Lorraine mayors agreed, for example, to remain
in their jobs under the Nazi boot. However, whatever the truth of
these portrayals, they rekindled above all the sentimental patriotism which, with Daudet or Hansi, had wept for the lost provinces
for some forty years. Likewise, the Resistance newspapers gave
great importance to supplies – a theme exploited again and again.
'We are only short of wine because we deliver our harvests to Germany' thundered *Combat*[27] for example. 'The Boches are pillaging
France' exclaimed *L'Humanité*.[28] And in a long article devoted to
'their pillage', *Résistance* detailed the losses inflicted by the Germans on the French economy.[29] Some fanciful rumours sometimes
added spice to the austerity of these figures. *Combat* asserted, for
example, that 'the Boches are circulating forged bank notes'.[30]
Resorting to these themes allowed the Resistance to orchestrate
popular discontent. By making the Germans responsible for
penury, the underground press offered a convenient explanation
which above all enabled the exasperation of civilians to be
directed towards an enemy all the more clearly identified for

25. *Défense de la France* nos. 1 (15 August 1941) and 5 (1941) (No. 5 has no more
precise date than this as the clandestine press did not always put the date on their
papers.)
26. 'L'Alsace reste française: elle lutte', *Franc-Tireur*, no. 12, October 1942.
27. 'Collaboration : pourquoi nous manquons de vin?', *Combat*, March 1942.
28. 'Les Boches pillent la France', *L'Humanité*, 3 June 1944.
29. 'Leur pillage', *Résistance*, no. 18, 13 October 1943.
30. 'La France au pillage', *Combat*, no. 41, February 1943.

being despised. Without being untruthful, however, this interpretation remained simplistic. For while the occupier comprehensively plundered France, other reasons (for example the disruption of commercial systems, worn-out equipment, underinvestment, etc.) contributed to the economic destitution of the country. Whether it was deliberate or not, this simplifying of the stakes opened up room for manoeuvre for the Resistance, which explains why they frequently returned to these themes.

Likewise, the underground press offered a positive image of the USSR. The fact that *L'Humanité* gave a flattering portrait of the Soviet Union is hardly surprising. The fact that more Right-wing newspapers showered praise on the Red Army might on the other hand be grounds for astonishment. 'The fact that we do not share Russia's political opinions', writes *Combat*, for example, 'is one more reason for us to pay tribute to its heroic army and its leaders'.[31] For its part, *Franc-Tireur* celebrated Stalingrad as 'the clearest, heaviest, bloodiest defeat of Hitler since the war started'.[32] 'Leningrad, Moscow, Stalingrad are still standing up to the invader. Soviet resistance on the Volga and in the Caucasus and the rout of Rommel are annihilating the huge German pincers opened out onto the Near East. FROM NOW ON HITLER IS ALONE' exclaimed *Libération (sud)*.[33] This glorification of the Soviet forces glossed over the ideological reality of the USSR in order to favour its warlike stance. To describe the heroism of the Red Army, the press used vocabulary which had been brought into play during the First World War – a vocabulary once familiar to authors and readers alike, whose use had been outlawed by the rapid defeat in 1940. However this vision corresponded to a tangible reality. The USSR had taken on an overwhelmingly large part of the war effort between 1941 and 1943. The relatively peripheral nature of the other theatres of operation (Africa and Asia) only intensified the interest which public opinion showed in the eastern front. Taking this as read, other reasons explain the interest shown by the Resistance in the exploits of the Red Army. The Russophilia of the French and memories of the retreat by Napoleon were an invitation to draw an eager parallel between the Great Army and the expected rout of the Wehrmacht. However by loyally recognising the Soviet victories while distancing themselves from Stalinist

31. 'Hommage à l'armée russe', *Combat*, March 1942 (no number).
32. *Franc-Tireur*, no. 15, 20 February 1943.
33. 'La France reprend sa place au combat', *Libération (sud)*, no. 19, 15 November 1942.

political options, the Right-wing newspapers hoped to escape the wrath of the PCF, the French Communist Party, which was always ready to condemn its opponents' anticommunism. All these factors were an invitation to overstate the importance given to the east, to the detriment of the other fronts: one way, no doubt, of raising the morale of civilians by scoffing at the so-called invincibility of an army trapped in the Russian Steppe.

Underground newspapers, finally, offered a positive image of the Resistance which did not always correspond with reality. Its strength was therefore overestimated. The readers of *Franc-Tireur* thus learned that 'Paris and Lyons, for example, from now on seem like those Balkan villages in a state of permanent rioting and constant plotting, where the overworked police investigate, make raids, carry out searches, make arrests, without ever stamping out this underground mobilisation, this never-ending plotting'.[34] *Combat* claimed to gather together in its 'civilian army' 'tens of thousands of French men and women' in August 1942.[35] Likewise, the Resistance aimed to present itself as a disciplined and organised group, respecting order. The short-lived liberation of Oyonnax, on 11 November 1943, was thus presented as a military operation. The vocabulary used by *Libération (sud)* (groups of men, troops, an army worthy of the name, leaders, columns, etc.)[36] or *Franc-Tireur* (patriots of the maquis, army, military leaders, a disciplined army, etc.)[37] showed this. One can understand why the Resistance press showered praise on the military value of that beggar army. 'The FFI (*Forces Françaises de l'Intérieur*, the overall name given to the Resistance groups within France in the Second World War) which, in the eyes of the uninformed, still appeared yesterday to be weak, scattered elements, let loose in the countryside and only good for firing at random in ambushes and for sabotaging a railway line, were suddenly seen, in the light of the fighting, to be a major force' exclaimed *Libération (nord)*, a group close to the Socialists, in 1944.[38] All the underground newspapers gave a prominent place to communiqués detailing the military operations of the Resistance[39]. The press, finally, made rash promises with regard to the population. Appeal-

34. 'La Résistance plus forte que jamais', *Franc-Tireur*, 6 May 1944.

35. *Combat*, no. 33, August 1942.

36. 'Oyonnax, nous voilà!', *Libération (sud)*, no. 37, 12 October 1943.

37. 'A Oyonnax, le 11 novembre, les gars du maquis ont tenu la ville', *Franc-Tireur*, 1 December 1943.

38. *Libération (nord)*, no. 190, 14 August 1944.

39. For example, 'Ils se battent, ils tiendront', *Franc-Tireur*, no. 29, 1 March 1944.

ing to the '*réfractaires*' (French citizens who refused to work in Germany during the Second World War) to join the Maquis, *Libération (sud)* reassured them. 'Don't worry. YOU WILL HAVE WEAPONS AND YOU WILL HAVE LEADERS'.[40] 'In every region, in every commune, set up fighting centres linked to each other. We shall then organise them and we shall arm them,' proposed for its part *Défense de la France*[41] when it had no resources to implement its policy.

Magnifying its own importance, overstating its military value, making promises it could not keep, the Resistance deserted the ground of information to make speeches giving a large role to exaggeration. Several reasons, it is true, were the basis for this strategy. By bluffing about its strength and about its resources, the shadow army presented itself as a credible structure, able to organise the French whom it was calling upon to fight. Likewise, by insisting on its earnestness and its military effectiveness, it launched a counterattack on enemy propaganda, which presented it in very black colours. 'The terrorist initiative is a Petiot affair multiplied by 1,000' stated for example *Le Matin*[42] which, describing an attack, did not hesitate to run as their headline 'the bandits of the Maquis are imitating the bloody behaviour of the Soviets. They have killed and buried seven policemen and a school-teacher.'[43] Matching propaganda with propaganda – since it praised the Resistance – and counterpropaganda with counter-propaganda – since it rebutted the official leaflets – the Resistance here renounced its need for truth. To enemy language which criminalised it, Resistance vocabulary opposed the image of a military (therefore organised) force, powerful (therefore effective) and large (therefore legitimate). Stressing the facts of an armoury which was sometimes modest (e.g., the accounts of the operations carried out by irregular soldiers and Partisans of Communist persuasion) strengthened the parallel with an army on campaign, scattering victorious communiqués during the course of its triumphs. However, this vocabulary and these examples were far from the reality, and the language here bore all the hallmark of bluff, of excess or of deceit.

40. 'Notre tâche', *Libération (sud)*, no. 10, 5 April 1942.
41. Indomitus (Philippe Viannay), 'Résister', *Défense de la France*, no. 29, 15 March 1943.
42. *Le Matin*, 17 March 1944.
43. *Le Matin*, 6 March 1944. The two references to *Le Matin* are taken from the paper by Vincent Chansel, 'L'image de la résistance dans la presse collaborationniste et vichyiste', *Memoir de l'Institut d'Etudes Politiques de Paris*, 1995, pp. 117-18.

The underground press thus used many different registers. To raise awareness and rally the population, to counter and refute the prevailing language, it used simultaneously and successively, informative or interpretative registers, while sometimes resorting to propaganda to cover up the true facts. However, was its language credible?

For lack of sources describing the way the underground press was received – and therefore the effects it had – the reply to this question has something of a mission impossible about it, even though several hypotheses can be suggested. Let us point out from the outset that Resistance newspapers resorted to various procedures to confer credibility on their message. Besides referring to the foreign media from time to time, they did not hesitate to bluff. *Franc-Tireur* refrained from numbering its first editions to avoid the ridicule of a single number,[44] and *Libération (sud)* presented itself without batting an eyelid as the 'Newspaper of the directorate of the French liberation forces'. The Resistance movements, moreover, developed subtle distribution strategies. To obtain a mass effect, *Défense de la France* flooded whole districts and streets. And on 14 July 1943, the movement of Philippe Viannay proceeded to distribute openly in the Paris Metro, an operation which was obviously spectacular and which aimed to show the strength of a movement able to operate in broad daylight. With this example, *Defense de la France* was inviting the French in concrete terms to 'free themselves from fear', a call which its newspaper hammered home.[45] It should also be made clear that the clumsiness and the extravagant language of enemy propaganda cancelled out what it was saying and validated, as a repercussion, the Resistance stance. Finally – and perhaps especially – the working methods of the underground press must have greatly contributed to legitimising its word, the value of the newspaper not depending solely on its content but on the very risk involved in producing and distributing forbidden papers.

In fact, the repressive authorities considered the Resistance newspapers to be a real danger. The distribution and production of secret leaflets were both punishable by heavy sanctions – in particular the death penalty.[46] And the Germans became alarmed

44. 'Nous aurons l'air de quoi si nous ne publions que le numéro un' declared Jean-Pierre Lévy to Antoine Avinin, quoted in *La Presse clandestine*, Paris, Cavaillon, 1986, p. 94.

45. For specific examples see Olivier Wieviorka, *Une Certaine Idée de la résistance. Défense de la France, 1940-1949*, Paris, Seuil, L'Univers historique, 1995, p.114.

46. German regulation of 18 December 1942, AN F60 1698.

about the possible effects of this seditious propaganda. 'Although the security of the country is not put in danger by anti-German propaganda, it creates an atmosphere in which people are disposed to fight against Germany, a fight which tends to get fiercer as economic and social hardships increase and the French grow more impatient. Combating this anti-German propaganda is a task of political significance' noted, for example, the *MilitärBefehlshaber in Frankreich* (German Military Commander in France). 'Numerous factors play a role in favour of maintaining an underground press' observed for their part the French police. 'Through their unanimously anti-German activity, the newspapers (...) continue to enjoy the sympathy of those whom they are reaching illegally (...). The simple fact that the so-called Gaullist newspapers attack the Government and make it responsible, with the Germans, for all the current evils, is sufficient to ensure for all these disparate documents a considerable number of informants, writers, sellers and readers. All these people see their illegal activity as continued participation in a war which they have never stopped believing to be just and finally victorious'[47].

Dreaded by the Germans and by the French State, was the underground press effective for all that? From an ideological point of view it no doubt contributed to the rejection of Vichy and the occupier, while consolidating a consensus around General de Gaulle. The immediate disqualification of the Pétain regime and the peaceful restoration of republican legality were not automatic. By legitimising the Resistance groups and the provisional government of General de Gaulle through its use of language, the Resistance press may well have spared France the sort of Civil War suffered by other countries, Greece in particular. It is not certain, on the other hand, whether it was newspapers that managed to mobilise the French. In the Vaucluse, for example, the calls to demonstrate launched by the Communist press on 1 and 11 November 1943 were not followed up,[48] radio being without a doubt a far more powerful weapon.

Because of the extent of its readership, on the other hand,[49] the underground press played a real part in creating three myths. By

47. Direction of the Sûreté, 'Les publications gaullistes éditées en France pendant l'année 1943', 18 January 1944, AN F1A 3758. (Translator's note: '*mots*' – words – in the original is obviously a misprint for '*maux*' – evils.)
48. Serge Issautier, 'La presse clandestine en Vaucluse pendant la Seconde guerre mondiale' in *La Presse Clandestine*, p. 44.
49. *Défense de la France* from October 1943 had a circulation of over 200,000 copies; *Le Populaire*, *L'Humanité* and *Combat* being, in 1944, at comparable levels.

offering a justified but idealised portrayal of the Red Army, it probably improved the image of the Soviet Union. In October 1944, 61 per cent of Parisians questioned by the *Institut Français d'Opinion Publique* considered, for example, that the USSR was the nation which had most contributed to German defeat,[50] a percentage which was confirmed by 57 per cent of those polled in Summer 1945.[51] And 83 per cent of the people interviewed were delighted by the alliance agreed between Paris and Moscow in December 1944.[52] The underground press moreover helped to create the image of a powerful, responsible and legitimate Resistance. In spite of General de Gaulle's reservations, for example, in the spring of 1945 70 per cent of French people wanted the government to take into consideration views expressed by the CNR[53] (*Conseil national de la Résistance* – the central organisation of the French Resistance). And more than 50 per cent believed that the *Comités départementaux de Libération* played a useful role.[54] On the other hand, as soon as the Resistance moved away from its political or military roles, public opinion rebelled. The breaking up of the patriotic Militia, with their ambiguous role, was therefore approved overwhelmingly (63 per cent).[55] And when the FFI engaged in dubious behaviour, they were violently attacked, a proof that the population did not intend to tolerate discrepancies appearing between the realities and the ideal portrayals fabricated by the underground press. 'Public opinion is extremely harsh towards [the FFI] and regrets their lack of discipline, their scruffy appearance and their lack of conscientiousness in performing certain tasks which had been entrusted to them' noted, for example, the Prefect of the Ain.[56] Finally, the underground press had legitimised the myth of a rapid return to prosperity. Developing the theme of German pillage, Radio London and the Resistance newspapers gave great credence to the idea that the departure of the Germans would be sufficient for a return to prewar affluence. 'Amongst the majority of the population there are high hopes of a rapid return to wellbeing' noted, for example the Prefect of the Ardèche.[57] And Alfred Sauvy deplored the fact that 'right up

50. *Bulletin de l'Institut Français d'Opinion Publique (IFOP)*, no. 1, 1 October 1944.
51. *Bulletin de l'IFOP*, 1 July 1945 (no number).
52. *Bulletin de l'IFOP*, no. 11, 1 March 1945.
53. *Bulletin de l'IFOP*, no. 14, 16 April 1945.
54. *Bulletin de l'IFOP*, no. 10, 16 February 1945.
55. *Bulletin de l'IFOP*, 1 December 1944 (no number).
56. Report from the Prefect of l'Ain, 18 January 1945, AN F1 CIII 1205.
57. Prefect of the Ardèche, report of 15 August 1945, AN F1CIII 1209.

to the last day, Radio Algiers retained the theme 'the Germans are taking everything', maintaining the most dangerous illusions'.[58]

Thus the secret press constantly swayed between propaganda and telling the truth. The plurality of its missions no doubt explains this tension between conflicting demands. Because it simultaneously had to convince public opinion, counter the words of the enemy, rally the French and justify its existence, the Resistance resorted to a variety of registers, informative, interpretative, propagandist. However, in spite of these opposite approaches, the message which the shadow army wanted to address to the French was not really confused. The disrepute of the official press, the collapse of Vichy power, the recognised prestige of General de Gaulle, all went to prove the effectiveness of a press which had honourably fulfilled its mission. Certainly, some questionable myths may have been fabricated along the way. By promising the immediate return of white bread and by extolling the virtues of the Red Army, it took some risks, it is true. The violent strikes in 1947-48 showed this. Overall, however – and the strength of these myths are a confirmation of this – the words of the Resistance struck home. Is it necessary to stress this? Its words were understood not least because they met with the implicit approval of a population worn out by the Vichy régime and crushed by four appalling years of Occupation.

Translated by Marlene Burt

58. Alfred Sauvy, *La vie économique des Français de 1939 à 1945*, Paris, Flammarion, 1978, p. 222.

7

HEROES AND MARTYRS

The Changing Mythical Status of the French Army
during the Indochinese War

Nicola Cooper

In Indochina, France's Fourth Republic experienced and lost its
first colonial war. If Algeria has been commonly perceived as '*la
guerre sans nom*',[1] the war without a name, then the Indochinese
conflict might well be termed '*la guerre occultée*', the overlooked, or
overshadowed war. Situated chronologically between two wars
which were to mark the French national *conscience, imaginaire* and
mémoire profoundly, and overshadowed by the traumatic American experience in Vietnam which followed it,[2] the Franco-Indochinese war was one which was conducted amidst profound

---

1. This epithet was coined by Bertrand Tavernier, in his film of the same name,
which appeared in 1992.

2. See Ramirez, F., and Rolot, C., 'D'Une Indochine à l'autre', *Cinémathèque* 2,
November 1992, pp. 40-55:

> *Le Viêt-nam et sa guerre ont, contre toute analyse et même contre tout bon sens, isolé l'Indochine
> dans un temps mythique et reculé. L'Indochine dans cet imaginaire-là, est désormais séparée du Viêt-
> nam un peu comme la Perse l'est de l'Iran. Elle est autre, coloniale et exotique, prête pour les regrets
> et les idéalisations* (p. 42).

> (Vietnam and the war there, despite rational analysis and even despite good sense, have
> isolated Indochina in a mythical past. Indochina, in this imagined conception, is forever dis-
> tinct from Vietnam, rather as Persia is forever distinct from Iran. It is other, colonial, exotic,
> a ready subject for regret and idealised portrayal.)

Metropolitan (mainland French) indifference,[3] and one which has received, and continues to receive very scant attention.

This may be due to the fact that the Indochinese war was unlike other wars in which France had been involved in the twentieth century. The Franco-Indochinese war was neither a struggle for national sovereignty and territory (as in the case of the two World Wars), nor was it a war which involved conscription to the French army. Neither did it provoke the same domestic tensions as the Algerian War which followed closely on its heels. It was a hybrid war, a war of changing focus and purpose; a national war of international dimensions.

Moreover, the French colonial relationship with Indochina had always been at best ambivalent. The furthest flung of all France's overseas territories, and separated from the Metropole by some four thousand kilometres, the various territories which came to make up French Indochina were annexed, appropriated, acquired and accrued over a period spanning some thirty years, from approximately 1860 to 1890. As many historians of French imperialism have noted, French expansionism did not form part of a coherent policy. This observation is all the more true in the case of Indochina. The French acquisition of Indochina resulted more from a series of individual and autonomous acts on the part of explorers, merchants and traders, than from intervention from Paris. Indochina's political boundaries were formally delimited in 1887, when the French government created the *Union Indochinoise*.

The nation's colonial role in Indochina can most usefully be summarised through a series of antitheses. In a variety of textual and visual media – colonial architecture, Metropolitan school manuals, colonial fiction, travel journalism, government literature and the writings of prominent colonial apologists – the Franco-Indochinese relationship was imagined and portrayed as generous yet self-seeking; liberatory yet authoritarian; modernising, yet encouraging the maintenance of Indochina in a 'primitive' or 'traditional' state. The relationship was simultaneously perceived as reciprocal and impositional, fostering development and yet a hindrance to autonomous cultural and political growth.[4]

---

3. See Alain Ruscio's work on the Franco-Indochinese war and public opinion: A. Ruscio, *La Guerre française d'Indochine*, Brussels, Editions Complexe, 1992; and 'French Public Opinion and the War in Indochina: 1945-54', in Scriven and Wagstaff, *War and Society in Twentieth Century France*, Oxford, Berg, 1991.

4. See my doctoral thesis 'French Discourses of Colonialism: the Case of French Indochina 1900-1939', University of Warwick, 1998.

Metropolitan representations and images of Indochina from the turn of the century onwards demonstrate a similarly antithetical discursive framework. Fraternal towards and respectful of Indochina under certain circumstances (the most notable demonstration being the Colonial Exhibition at Vincennes in 1931, where a replica of the Cambodian temples of Angkor physically dominated the exhibition ground in an attempt to impress upon visitors the beneficial action of French colonialism), imperial France sought also to express her superiority and control over her colonised peoples of Asia. Valorised as '*la perle de l'Extrême-Orient*', Indochina was France's rival to Britain's 'jewel in the crown': advanced, worthy, and accorded special status. Indochina was nevertheless chaotic and weak, inferior and needy. Indochina was a showcase of success, but also a site of disaster. Indochina was singled out and praised, but was also denied specificity, both internally and in relation to France's other colonial possessions. Praised and held up as a shining example of the value of French colonialism, Indochina was simultaneously diminished, commodified and debased.

It is interesting to note that many of the discourses of French colonialism, the ideals of Empire, and their application to Indochina, remained constant throughout the Franco-Indochinese relationship. Indeed, the end of the colonial relationship, played out upon the battleground of Dien Bien Phu, is of interest as it is a period in which French imperial discourses of earlier decades are put to the test and finally reiterated, if in a somewhat diluted form. The front covers of *Paris Match*, which will be the principal focus of this chapter, depict the French retreat from its Indochinese Empire and provide an ambiguous conclusion to the period of French colonisation in Indochina. Whilst the anti-colonial Metropolitan voice, so marked in its absence from the views of the Franco-Indochinese relationship of the 1920s and 1930s had been swelling during the nine years of war between France and Indochina, 'the end of the Indochinese dream' was nevertheless marked by visual and textual discourses which alluded frequently to the tenets of colonialism which had sustained French rule in Indochina for some ninety years.

Although contemporary domestic preoccupations with questions of national security (the fear of German rearmament most notably) inevitably drew attention away from this distant colonial conflict, it is the consistent ambivalence of the Franco-Indochinese relationship that appears to figure as the principal reason why this war was and continues to be largely overlooked in France. Whereas less than a decade later, the Algerian War would become an acutely felt domestic as well as colonial problem, the popular response to the Indochinese war, one essentially of well-documented indifference, is a measure of mainland France's tenuous affective link with Indochina.

This question of Indochina's status, and its place within the French Empire, can be linked, with the onset of war, to the perception of the French army's role and duty. In previous conflicts of the twentieth century, war had been perceived as a glorious duty. The Third Republic had, through its preoccupation with civil, moral and military education, prepared generations of male citizens for whom their first duty was to *la patrie*, and for whom death in the name of *la patrie* was a glorious honour: blood shed in order to save the nation.

The goals of these previous wars were (superficially at least) clearly defined: the Motherland was threatened, national independence was at stake. The Indochinese war on the other hand, had ill-defined goals, and an often 'invisible' enemy. In its representation of its actions in 1945-46, official France drew on the same myths and discourses which had characterised its initial justification of the conquest of Indochina, in its attempt to square its actions in Asia with both the international community, and the home population. Throughout the period of administrative and governmental consolidation in Indochina (ie: roughly 1900s-1930s) France's role in Indochina was imagined through discourses of protection and generosity. The narrative of conquest was rewritten in history books as a reactive gesture of altruistic intent, carried out in response to often unspecific 'troubles', 'encroachments', and 'problems'.

Although in 1945-46 the Indochinese conflict clearly seemed to be a war of reconquest, it was, however, perceived successively as a 'liberation' from Japanese control, protection from the potentially acquisitive desires of the British troops who oversaw the capitulation of the Japanese in Indochina, and from the increasing menace of Chinese and Russian intervention. This myth of liberation is embodied in the choice of General Leclerc, liberator of Paris, as the first commanding officer to oversee the expeditionary French forces in Indochina.

When, towards the end of the war, General de Castries observed the *'distance profonde'* ('the great gulf') which separated what was at stake for the Viet Minh and what was at stake for the French forces:

'entre une armée nationale se battant sur son sol et pour l'indépendance de sa patrie, et une armée de métier faisant honneur à son contrat',[5] ('between a national army fighting on its own territory for its own national independence, and a professional army honouring its contract') he could just as well have been talking about the differences between the previous wars France had fought in the twentieth century, and the conflict in which it was now embroiled. The *patrie*, the Fatherland, was not in danger; there seemed little connection between domestic concerns and this distant conflict. Confusion as to the role of the army, or indeed the role and interests of France in Southeast Asia seemed to have come full circle. Just as in the 1880s, Indochina was perceived as wasteful of *'l'or et le sang de la France'*[6] ('French gold and French blood').

The encampment at Dien Bien Phu was created on the orders of General Navarre in November 1953, and situated at the extreme West of Tonkin, on the border with Laos. It was constructed in response to rumours that Giap's forces were heading towards Laos. The decision was therefore taken to create a *'verrou'*, a 'bolt' which would ensure the control of the sole main road to Laos, thus preventing passage from Tonkin to Laos.

Mirroring French representations of France's role in Indochina since the conquest, Dien Bien Phu was envisaged as a protective and reactive gesture. Sixteen kilometres in length, the military camp was constructed inside a huge basin, surrounded by fortified hillsides. Inside the basin a runway was built to ensure supply routes to the camp. Hundreds of troops were parachuted in to secure the camp, which totalled 11,000 men.

It had been calculated that Giap would need from five to seven months to arm and supply himself sufficiently to mount an attack on the camp. French Command believed that Giap had insufficient troops to deploy in the area, his main bases were far away, and French fire power significantly outweighed Vietnamese artillery and fire power. Moreover, Giap would have to mobilise a significant section of the local population to ensure that supplies and arms were transported to Dien Bien Phu, by a stream of lorries, bicycles, and coolies on foot. No one believed the Vietnamese would dare to attack such a seemingly impregnable and unassailable fortress.

---

5. De Castries, quoted in Rocolle, P., (Colonel), *Pourquoi Dien Bien Phu?*, Paris, Flammarion, 1968.

6. This metaphor was first used in relation to Indochina during the period of conquest and pacification, and became one of the principal arguments of the anti-expansionists in the parliamentary debates on colonialism of the 1880s.

By December 1953, however, the camp had been encircled by Giap's troops. On 13 March 1954 Giap's troops attacked. After heavy shelling, two of the advance hilltop positions were immediately taken: Béatrice and Gabrielle. By 17 March, the runway had been so severely damaged as to be impracticable, and a further post, Anne-Marie, had been lost. Dien Bien Phu was in fact a monumental miscalculation.

As a response to a humiliating defeat, the mythology of Dien Bien Phu now commenced in earnest, and, as I hope to suggest, underwent a series of shifts and refocusings, as the French nation attempted to come to terms with news of events at Dien Bien Phu, the first serious assault which threatened colonial rule, and which was to lead ultimately to the loss of France's first colonial war.

Despite the seizure of important strategic locations around the basin at Dien Bien Phu, the French press initially remained buoyant. This confidence is reflected in the emphasis which was placed on the historical significance of the battle of Dien Bien Phu. The press was full of references to textualising and contextualising narratives of glory and success:

Ils écrivent une page de gloire dans le ciel de Dien Bien Phu[7] ('They are writing a glorious page in the skies of Dien Bien Phu').

Les héroiques défenseurs de Dien Bien Phu écrivent un magnifique chapitre de l'histoire militaire française[8] ('The heroic defenders of Dien Bien Phu are writing a magnificent chapter of French military history').

The media consistently invoked a sense of history, and historical continuity around the battle, inventing a tradition of military glory for Metropolitan France, and thereby adding weight, significance and depth to a conflict which scarcely interested the majority of the French public.

The need for a worthy point of comparison was found in the mythology of the First World War: Dien Bien Phu became: *'Le Verdun tropical'*[9] ('the Verdun of the Tropics'), *'le Verdun de la brousse'*[10] ('the Verdun of the bush'), *'le Verdun de la jungle'*[11] ('the Verdun of the jungle'), *'le Verdun tonkinois'*[12] ('the Verdun of Tonkin'). Certain physical conditions at Dien Bien Phu bore some resemblance to

7. *Paris Match*, 3 April 1954.
8. John Foster Dulles, quoted in *L'Aurore*, 24 March 1954.
9. *Le Figaro*, 15 April 1954.
10. *Paris Match*, 10 April 1954.
11. *L'Aurore*, 6 May 1954.
12. *Progrès de Lyon*, 2 April 1954.

the conditions at Verdun: the proximity of the two sides, the violence, the existence of trenches, the huge bomb craters, the ubiquitous mud, etc. But more importantly, Verdun was of course an idealised battle, embodying, in Poincaré's words, *'ce qu'il y a de plus beau, de plus pur et de meilleur dans l'âme française. Il est devenu synonyme synthétique de patriotisme, de bravoure et de générosité'*[13] ('what is most beautiful, purest and best in the French soul. It has become a synomym for patriotism, bravery and generosity of spirit combined').

Dien Bien Phu was thus initially envisaged as occupying a glorious place in the annals of French military history, a successor to Verdun, and also as embodying perceived national values, principles and attributes: patriotism, courage and generosity, all of which had permeated colonial discourses throughout the 1920s and 1930s.

As it became clearer that the French forces were losing their grip in Indochina, and defeat became probable as opposed to a possible, press reporting gave rise to two thematic *topoi*: the representation of French defeats, through a slippage of language, as *'foudroyantes contre-attaques'*[14] ('stunning counterattacks'); and the hysterical treatment of the Viet Minh in the French media, drawing on colonial and racist discourses: *'innombrables masses jaunes'* ('innumerable yellow hordes'), *'vagues hurlantes'*[15] ('roaring waves'), *'masses fanatisées'*[16] ('fanatical hordes'), *'soldats endoctrinés'*[17] ('indoctrinated troops'): savage drunken masses who fired upon Red Cross vehicles and refused to allow French casualties to be evacuated from Dien Bien Phu.

These are both standard rhetorical devices employed to 'explain away', and to deflect attention from military setbacks. They were used to discredit and devalorise the enemy as inhuman, fanatical, merciless, and in turn allowed for a further shift in press representation. For if the heroes of the French army were not fighting an enemy who adhered to the 'rules of the game', international military convention, then the war itself was not being fairly fought, nor fairly won by the Viet Minh. The French heroes

13. Quoted in Prost, A., 'Verdun', in Nora, P., *Les Lieux de la mémoire: La Nation III*, Paris, Gallimard, 1986.

14. *France-Soir*, 30 March 1954, carried as its headline: 'Foudroyante contre-offensive française à Dien Bien Phu'.

15. *Le Populaire*, 1 April 1954.

16. *France-Soir*, 1 April 1954.

17. *Le Figaro*, 23 January 1954.

became martyrs, their defeat *'un calvaire'*[18] ('a calvary'). The arrogant tone of the first months of 1954 was thus gradually abandoned in favour of a new theme: heroic martyrdom.

This evolution of representation was played out most visibly in *Paris Match* through the magazine's extensive use of photography. *L'Aurore* of 24 March published the first photographs of the battle, but it was *Paris Match* which became the specialist of war photography. From 20 March to 15 May it published 144 photos of the battle, of which five were front covers.

Although the series of photographs which *Paris Match* published inside its covers would be a fertile ground for analysis, the front covers themselves are perhaps more interesting as they attempt to convey, in a single image, the *essence* of Dien Bien Phu to the readership. Whilst the numerous shots of the battlefield, the parachutists, the HQ, the trenches, etc. etc., which appeared inside the magazine, present a teleological vision of the war, a progression, albeit a progression which moves from possible victory to potential defeat, the front covers on the other hand, attempt to distil an exemplary image, to create an archetype, to formulate what we would term a myth of the French army.

If, as Barthes noted of the African colonial soldier saluting the tricolore in a later *Paris Match* front cover, *'il est la présence même de l'impérialité française'*[19] ('he is the very embodiment of French imperialism'), then what these photographs signify is perhaps *'la présence d'une impérialité française souffrante'* ('the embodiment of suffering French imperialism'), but I would add, *'souffrante, mais pas encore mourante'* ('suffering, but not yet dying').

The myth of Dien Bien Phu was accompanied by the headlines: *'la tragédie des blessés'*[20] ('the tragedy of the wounded'), *'le calvaire et la gloire du Général de Castries'*[21] ('the moral agony and glory of General de Castries'), *'l'épopée de Dien Bien Phu'*[22] ('the epic of Dien Bien Phu'). Tragedy and suffering are thus offset by the glory, and the epic quality of the battle. French colonialism is undergoing severe pressure, but its principles remain untarnished, undiminished.

However, these new representations demonstrate the difficulty, the discomfort produced by the attempt simultaneously to represent heroism, or undiminished national grandeur alongside defeat.

18. This term was in fact used as a headline in one of *Paris Match*'s front covers.
19. Barthes, R., *Mythologies*, Paris, Seuil, (1957) 1970, p. 214.
20. *Paris Match*, 22 May 1954.
21. *Paris Match*, 13 May 1954.
22. *Paris Match*, 8 May 1954.

In his mythical capacity, the warrior is valour, energy, idealism, and masculinity at its zenith. He is fearsome and venerable; a man of exceptional courage, valour and steadfastness, who is given to acts of bravery. In these photographs the warrior is agonised, despairing, exhausted, mutilated, the protected rather than the protector. The hero in these photographs has been transmuted into heroism's close but significantly more vulnerable partner: the martyr.

In the arena of war, heroism and martyrdom have often become blurred in this way, and the hero has often been embodied by common man, elevated by sacrifice to the status of hero or martyr: the *poilu* of the First World War being the most enduring model of this traditional paradigm. His passage to heroism is marked by resistance in the face of overwhelming odds, his resilience when overwhelmed by appalling physical conditions. His glory and his heroism are achieved through the transgression of the limits of the human condition, which in defeat or death marks his ultimate passage to martyrdom. This heroism of the common man can be translated as dogged determination to carry out one's perceived duty to a higher good, usually the good of the nation. It is 'not deserting', 'not leaving one's post' – '*ils ont tenu*' ('they stood their ground'), rather than '*ils ont vaincu*' ('they conquered').

Certainly, the soldiers at Dien Bien Phu '*ont tenu*'. Both photographs and journalism of the period bear witness to the fortitude and steadfastness of the beleagured French army: bomb craters, wounded men remaining at their posts in the trenches. As Jean-Marie Garraud reported in *Le Figaro* of 5 April:

> *Depuis 120 heures, accrochés à leurs pointes d'appui, au milieu de la poussière et de la fumée des incendies, dans le fracas des explosions, ces hommes résistent magnifiquement aux furieux assauts d'un ennemi cinq fois supérieur en nombre. Malgré la fatigue, l'insomnie, la chaleur, ils tiennent dans leurs tranchées, aux créneaux de leurs postes, les mains crispés sur leurs armes.*

> (For 120 hours, covered in dust and smoke, amid the tumult of continuous explosions, these men stayed at their posts and put up a magnificent resistance to the assaults of an enemy force five times their number. Despite their fatigue, their lack of sleep, and the great heat, they held on in their trenches and at their look-out posts, with their weapons at the ready.)

However, and to return to a point I made briefly at the beginning of this chapter, the French forces in Indochina consisted of professional soldiers. In the Indochinese conflict, the myth of the heroic common man no longer applies. These myths of soldierly heroism are diminished and devalued when the men in question are professional soldiers, *engagés*. To recall de Castries, these men *'faisaient honneur à leur contrat'* ('were honouring their contract'). Neither does the image of the French forces presented by *Paris Match* accurately reflect their composition in reality. In 1952 the composition of the French forces in Indochina was as follows: 54,000 French; 30,000 North Africans; 18,000 Africans; 20,000 Légionnaires; 53,000 natives; 50,000 members of the Vietnamese national army; 15,000 members of the Laotian army; 10,000 members of the Cambodian army.[23]

While at a later date it was useful to represent French colonial interests by the association of a uniformed negro with the national flag, here the army is very clearly portrayed as white and western. A portrayal which is clearly at odds with the reality. Whilst the *ralliement*, the rallying of troops of colonial origin to the aid of the Motherland in the First World War had been publicised and lauded, the Indochinese war appears to be represented, in spite of the army's reliance on colonial troops, as an exclusively Metropolitan affair. In the face of defeat by a colonised people, the French press redrew the battle lines along racial grounds. The French army was depicted as just that. A French army.

Additionally, the Indochinese war was, more than any other war involving twentieth-century France, a conflict which came to be represented from within a framework of French aristocratic dimensions. The two figures who feature prominently on these *Paris Match* covers are General de Castries and Geneviève de Galard. Their names themselves are indicators of an aristocratic descent.

Indeed, much colonial thought of the 1920s and 1930s focuses on aristocratic values, and what I have termed elsewhere the myth of *'autrefois'*: an unspecified period, a 'golden age' of French colonialism. The dynamic of this myth of *'autrefois'* nostalgically imagines French Indochina as the last outpost in which aristocratic values have survived. The colonist, innately superior by birth, nationality and class, commands immediate respect from his underlings through his very bearing and demeanour. Those critical of contemporary colonial management in Indochina regretted the passing of this mythical period of harmony and social integrity, and sought to recuperate and reinstate this lost

23. Figures from P.-M. de la Gorce, *The French Army : A military-political History*, London, Weidenfeld and Nicolson, 1963, trans. K. Douglas.

golden age of distance, hierarchy and authority between colonised and coloniser.[24]

The front cover depicting General de Castries, a former cavalry officer, signals the final death of the aristocratic colonial tradition in Indochina, and perhaps the aristocratic tradition of the French army itself. For it was during this post-Second World War period that the army underwent a *dégagement des cadres*, which effectively reduced the numbers of senior officers in the army by up to 45 per cent. Graduates from the military schools became a minority, and thus those of a bourgeois or aristocratic background became far less numerous, and increasingly officers rose from within the ranks of the regular army.[25] Thus in the immediate postwar period, the forces underwent a form of enforced democratisation, which was at odds with its traditionally perceived image of the French national army.

Seen from the context of the Indochinese war, however, de Castries' portrait (Figure 8) signals the hopelessness of the French position. His is not the imperious gaze of a commanding officer confident of his troops. Bereft of his dress uniform, de Castries is allied not with his class, his ancestors and his political superiors at home: he is very firmly placed alongside his troops, he is 'one of them'. His photograph foretells the rift whose seeds were sown in Indochina, but only came to bear fruit in Algeria, between the 'men on the ground', the serving soldiers, and the general staff, the politicians at home. De Castries is portrayed on the side of the heroic combatants against the traitors at home.

Geneviève de Galard, both aristocratic and a heroine, captured popular French imagination and became the darling of the French press. Galard was rapidly nicknamed by the popular press, – *'l'ange de Dien Bien Phu'* ('the angel of Dien Bien Phu') – and enjoyed several weeks of great celebrity, figuring on the front page of *Paris Match*, *France Soir* and *Le Figaro*. It was exceptional that a woman remained, right until the end, at the entrenched camp.[26] But this is not simply the portrait of a courageous nurse from *'la France pro-*

24. See the work of travel journalists to Indochina in the 1930s: in particular, Viollis, A., *SOS Indochine*, Paris, Gallimard, 1935; and Roubaud, L., *Vietnam : la tragédie indochinoise*, Paris, Valois, 1931.

25. Statistics from de la Gorce, *The French Army*.

26. In fact Geneviève de Galard was not the sole woman remaining in the French camp. There were several prostitutes, sent from Hanoi, some of whom were killed during the bombings. Some of them acted as nurses, although no mention of them was to be found in the press at the time.

Figure 8 *General de Castries,* Paris Match *front cover, 1954*

fonde' ('the heart of France'). De Galard becomes an icon because she is de Galard, a woman of aristocratic background. She is an appropriate and worthy figure to tend the wounded French troops.

It is, at first glance, and discounting the 'human interest' angle, somewhat surprising that the press should have seized upon Geneviève de Galard to epitomise the French experience at Dien Bien Phu. Although it has become a standard reflex to observe that war exorcises the feminine, that war is a masculinised domain *par excellence,* a homosocial institution, it is nevertheless striking that media attention attached itself so firmly to a female figure at this point in the Franco-Indochinese war, for the feminine had been rigorously excluded from representations of Indochina until this point. Women, and more particularly female Metropolitan settlers, had been marginalised and vilified in Metropolitan literature on Indochina. In both popular and official texts, Indochina had been imagined as a male haven; a domain for male action, permeated with qualities such as virility, energy and courage.

This male (and essentially aristocratic) haven was shattered by the arrival of European women in Indochina in the 1920s. Representations of this period contrast activity with passivity; theory with practice; a consumerist, egotistical and 'feminine' society, with a pioneering, selfless and 'masculine' one. Texts praise the warrior-like qualities of an elite male order, contrasting this chivalric fraternal community with a feminised bureaucracy. The idyllic era of the heroic and aristocratic male *broussard* (European settler living in the 'bush') was corrupted and undermined by the literal and metaphorical feminisation of the colony.

De Galard's role was undoubtedly sentimentalised and therefore diminished by the press: *Le Figaro* of 6 May revealed that the French soldiers had nicknamed her *'Bécassine'*,[27] *'à cause de son visage rond presque celui d'un bébé, [qui] garde, quelles que soient les circonstances, un calme extraordinaire et ne trahit aucune émotion'* ('because of her round, almost babyish face, which stays extraordinarily calm and betrays no emotion, whatever the circumstances').

Similarly, *Paris Match* of 1 May noted: *'la seule douceur des blessés : le sourire de Geneviève'* ('the only solace of the wounded: Geneviève's smile'). But de Galard is also the epitome of what Metropolitan France imagined the woman settler in Indochina should be: useful, dutiful, practical. She embodies activity rather than passivity.

The portrait of de Galard (Figure 9) shows her in her nurse's uniform, looking straight at the lens. It is an accessible, open expression; she is a cheerful, capable figure. In Figure 10, de Galard is caught in action, loading a wounded soldier onto a truck. Here she appears as a comrade in battle. Directing the men around her, she is clearly in charge. The woman striding across the runway in the last photo (Figure 11) is purposeful, businesslike and, from the expression, serenely confident despite being the focus of much attention from the group behind.

Indeed, this photograph represents her as a somewhat androgynous figure: dressed in combat uniform, she is viewed and observed, sexualised, but respected at the same time. Photographed from both front and behind as she walks, and clearly the object of male sexual attention (note the stance of the barechested male figures in the background), her gaze is nonetheless directed at the soldier to the right of the picture who stands to attention as she passes.

27. Bécassine is the main character of a popular French cartoon book for children, dating originally from the second decade of the century. Bécassine, who indeed has the round, smooth face of a baby, is a naive and rather silly young girl of Breton peasant stock who goes into service with an aristocratic family.

Figure 9 *Geneviève de Galard in nurse's uniform,* Paris Match *front cover, 1954*

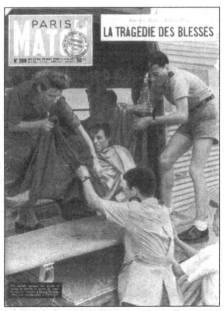

Figure 10 *Geneviève de Galard loading wounded soldiers,* Paris Match *front cover, 1954*

Figure 11 *Geneviève de Galard in combats,* Paris Match *front cover, 1954*

These almost paradoxical significations surrounding de Galard might be related to the type of fantasy of the female on the battlefield popularised by the novel/film *For Whom the Bell Tolls*, in which Hemingway's heroine represents the warrior's ideal mate: equally good with a gun or inside a sleeping bag. The woman in uniform (either nurse's or combat) is both slightly dishevelled and sexually inviting. Her sleeves rolled up in anticipation of action, de Galard nonetheless remains impeccably coiffured.

It is tempting to interpret these photographic images as yet another representation of the gendered and familial configuration of the Franco-Indochinese relationship, and even more tempting to see the Franco-Indochinese relationship as having come full circle: the infantilised colony rejects the parental control of France; the protective Motherland arrives at the moment of defeat to tend to her biological as opposed to her adopted children. But Geneviève de Galard also takes on something of a mythical status at Dien Bien Phu. Her name recalls Geneviève, the patron saint of Paris and protector of the capital, and de Galard can, perhaps more convincingly, be viewed as a Marianne figure, the embodiment of the protective Motherland but also a symbolic substitute for the emasculated Republic: a defeated France, unable to regain authority in the colony, and unable to defeat the previously derided enemy of *'les petits jaunes'* ('little yellow men').

By way of offering some preliminary steps towards a conclusion, these images convey the confusion with which the French press viewed events in Indochina. Dien Bien Phu represented *'la tragédie des blessés'* ('the tragedy of the wounded'), but was not *'une blessure tragique'* ('a tragic wound'). Dien Bien Phu was presented as an epic battle, but one with a vanquished hero. The reality of Dien Bien Phu was clearly humiliating – for the French army, and for the France as an imperial nation. This humiliation is mitigated however, through an attempt to demonstrate that although France had lost control of Indochina, her imperial principles, the values of *'la mission civilisatrice'* ('the civilising mission') – generosity, protection and an innate sense of national and racial 'aristocracy' – remained undiminished. They were epitomised by the steadfastness of the French troops, the courage of Geneviève de Galard, the torment of de Castries. One might wish to suggest that it was the very persistence and durability of these myths which led to the devastating and protracted trauma of Algeria.

8

A LA RECHERCHE DU SOLDAT PERDU

Myth, Metaphor, and Memory in The French Cinema of The Algerian War

Philip Dine

> Nations, like narratives, lose their origins in the myths of time and
> only fully realise their horizons in the mind's eye. Such an image of
> the nation – or narration – might seem impossibly romantic and
> excessively metaphorical, but it is from those traditions of political
> thought and literary language that the nation emerges as a power-
> ful historical idea in the west. An idea whose cultural compulsion
> lies in the impossible unity of the nation as a symbolic force.[1]

Amongst western nations, France is perhaps the one in which
Homi Bhabha's 'impossible unity' has been most regularly and
most visibly subjected to almost unbearable strain. For the 1789
Revolution which gave birth to the modern Republic was the
product of a great schism in French society which has regularly
resurfaced at moments of domestic and/or international
upheaval. Such variously spectacular outbursts of Franco-French
hostility as the Vendée wars, the Paris Commune, the Dreyfus
Affair, Vichy, and the events of May-June 1968 thus conform to a
pattern of regular threats to the modern nation-state's most basic
political, administrative, and security structures. Moreover, such
periodic explosions also regularly challenge its foundation myth,
the idea of 'the one and indivisible Republic'. This myth was only
transformed into an effective political reality under the ruthlessly

---

1. Homi K. Bhabha (ed.), *Nation and Narration*, London, Routledge, 1990, p. 1.

centralising regime of the Third Republic (1870-1940), which, as Eugen Weber has noted, embarked on a campaign of internal colonisation which swept away rural diversity in the name of a sacralised (and, of course, centralised and urbanised) unitary national culture.[2] It was this second republican 'supermyth' of French civilisation, of France's unique gift to a variously benighted world, which provided the cornerstone of Jacobin universalism, and which would be appealed to in the later nineteenth and early twentieth centuries to justify a 'civilising mission' which was to see France extend its overseas empire throughout the Maghreb, much of sub-Saharan Africa, and Indo-China.

Algeria, invaded in 1830, but not durably 'pacified' until the defeat of Abd-el-Kader, the leader of the indigenous resistance, in 1847, was France's first and most important colony. In 1848 it was destined to be reconfigured by French colonialism in a uniquely durable and damaging fashion. In a move which has its echoes in the experience of Ireland – England's oldest, most integrated, and most mythified, colony – Algeria was magically transformed by administrative decree into three *départements* of the Republic. Henceforth, Algeria would not be dealt with by the Ministry of the Colonies, still less by that of Overseas Affairs: the territory became mythically fixed as 'French Algeria', an integral province of the Republic just like Brittany, Alsace, or, for that matter, Corsica. As the decolonising 'winds of change' swept through the French empire in the wake of the Second World War, just as they did through those of the other European colonial powers, it thus fell to successive Ministers of the Interior to explain why Algeria could not and would not be granted independence. Neither the experience of eight years of futile anti-insurrectionary warfare in France's principal Southeast Asian territory, Indo-China, nor even the army's ultimate and catastrophic defeat in that theatre served to shake the convictions of French politicians or French soldiers. Coming barely six months after the French army's humiliation at Dien Bien Phu, the uprising launched by the *Front de libération nationale* (FLN, the National Liberation Front) on All Saints' Day, 1 November 1954, would be met by a determined effort to use French military might to block what proved to be unstoppable Algerian political forces. As Pierre Mendès-France's Minister of the Interior, the young François Mitterrand, was to put it in justifying

2. Eugen Weber, *Peasants into Frenchmen: The Modernization of Rural France, 1870-1914*, London, Chatto and Windus, 1977, p. 98.

the conscription and mobilisation of young Frenchmen to serve in the conflict (a step that was, significantly, never taken during the war in Indo-China): *'L'Algérie, c'est la France'* ('Algeria is France').[3] The strategic colonial myths of the civilising mission and French Algeria thus combined with the republican foundation myth of the one and indivisible Republic to provide a justification for sending an army of, in total, over two and a half million 'soldier-citizens' (another important republican myth) to fight in Algeria. These key elements in the French nation's narration of its Algerian experience would be joined by a whole raft of tactical myths as France sought desperately to cling on to its most extensively settled, most economically integrated, and, above all, most symbolically and psychologically assimilated territory. The result was nothing less than what Jacques Duquesne identified as early as 1958 as 'the war of myths'.[4] Of these, the myth of the war's nonexistence is by far the most important. How, after all, could the indivisible Republic admit to being embroiled in a war of national liberation with three of its own *départements*? To admit to the existence of the conflict *qua* war was to explode the juridical myth of Algeria's 'provincial' status and thus to acknowledge the possibility of the 'natives' achieving independence there, just as they had achieved it through force of arms in Indo-China in 1954, and would shortly be granted it under relatively peaceful circumstances in Morocco and Tunisia, as well as in France's territories in sub-Saharan Africa.

There thus arose a wide range of official euphemisms by which the guerrilla war could safely be described: the Algerian 'events', the Algerian 'problem', the Algerian 'dispute'. For their part, the FLN's combatants were variously dismissed as 'criminals', 'bandits', 'outlaws', 'terrorists', or, most commonly, *'fellagha'*, a pejorative term originally meaning 'road-cutters' but which quickly became associated with 'throat-cutters', as the demonised nationalists were often represented by the French press. The army's mission, meanwhile, became the reassuring one of 'ensuring security', 'maintaining order', and, that mantra of colonial repression, 'pacification'. Thus was born the myth of 'the war without a name', as a veil not so much of silence as of false consciousness was drawn

3. See John Talbott, *The War Without a Name: France in Algeria, 1954-1962*, London, Faber and Faber, 1981, p. 39.

4. Jacques Duquesne, *L'Algérie ou la guerre des mythes*, Paris, Desclée de Brouwer, 1958.

by the French policy-making elite over the hostilities in Algeria. Finding an effective means of piercing this veil was to become a major preoccupation for opposition groups, intellectuals, and writers as revelations about the brutal reality of the war began to emerge, in spite of severe government censorship, in the wake of the so-called 'Battle of Algiers' (September 1956 to September 1957). Tales of mass arrests, torture, and summary execution could not easily be suppressed in a country which had, barely a decade earlier, itself been subjected to similarly abhorrent methods by an occupying army. Thus arose a new way of talking about the conflict: it was *'la sale guerre'*, a 'dirty war' characterised on the one hand by *'la gégène'* and *'le bain'* (respectively, torture by electrical shocks or immersion in water), and on the other by *'la corvée de bois'* ('woodcutting duties' from which Algerian 'suspects' would never return). The resulting polemic regarding the conduct and continuation of the war served to split Metropolitan French public opinion along its age-old fault-lines and has led commentators to describe the Algerian conflict variously as 'this new Dreyfus Affair', as a 'war of petitions', and, most memorably, as a 'battle of the written word'.[5] Manifestos, memoirs, articles, essays, and literary fictions would thus all be pressed into service as the intellectual guardians of French civilisation turned their patent version of that myth against those who sought to justify brutal methods of repression in Algeria in its name.

But what of non-print representations of the war in an increasingly audio-visual age? In the event, the treatment of Algeria was to fall somewhere between the French press's highly selective reporting of Indo-China – epitomised by the celebrated, and straightforwardly mythmaking, *Paris-Match* shots of the army's heroic last stand at Dien Bien Phu – and the virtually blanket coverage provided by American television of its own army's campaign against President Ho Chi Minh and General Vo Nguyen Giap a decade or so later, during the world's first 'living-room war' in Vietnam. While television was to become significantly more accessible in France during the late 1950s and early 1960s,

5. Bernard Droz, 'Le cas très singulier de la guerre d'Algérie', *Vingtième Siècle*, no.5 (special number on 'Les guerres franco-françaises', January-March 1985), pp. 81-90; Jean-François Sirinelli, 'Guerre d'Algérie, guerre des pétitions?', in Jean-Pierre Rioux and Jean-François Sirinelli (eds), *La Guerre d'Algérie et les intellectuels français*, Brussels, Editions Complexe, 1991, pp. 265-306; Michel Crouzet, 'La Bataille des intellectuels français', *La Nef*, nos. 12-13 (October 1962-January 1963), pp. 47-65.

the limited coverage provided of the Algerian conflict was to be straightforwardly propagandist in nature. Thus, on the one hand, reassuring images of the 'pacification' effort were provided by the current affairs magazine *Cinq colonnes à la une*; while, on the other, General de Gaulle was famously one of the first politicians successfully to exploit the new medium's power of persuasion in dramatic appeals to the public in mainland France (also broadcast by radio in France and Algeria) at moments of high drama such as the attempted military *putsch* in April 1961. The Algerian 'battle of the written word' thus became, at least periodically, 'the battle of the transistors'.

It might have been expected, or at least hoped, that film, a medium which France had done so much to develop, would have had a leading role to play in representing the Algerian conflict. For the French film industry had consistently been at the forefront, both as regards technical and artistic innovations: from the Lumière brothers, through Pathé, the poetic realism of the 1930s, the 'Tradition of Quality' fostered by the postwar *Centre National de la Cinématographie*, right up to the just now breaking New Wave. Surely such a great national cinema would have been to the fore in the very necessary process of demystifying the Algerian War: 'After all, one of the most important qualities of the medium of film as such, it is often claimed, lies in its very capacity to make visible, and to record events as they happen.'[6] Or, to put it another way, as does Bruno Forrestier, a young deserter from the Algerian War, in Jean-Luc Godard's second major film, *Le Petit Soldat* (The Little Soldier): 'Photography is the truth. Cinema is the truth twenty-four times a second'.

Ironically, the history of *Le Petit Soldat* itself provides an eloquent rebuttal to all such claims. Although produced in 1960 – the same year as Godard's epoch-making feature *A bout de souffle* (Breathless) (1960) – this work was deemed to be damaging to the French army in Algeria, and was consequently refused certification until 1963, and thus effectively banned from French cinema screens for the duration of the conflict. The censors' thwarting of this particular aspect of Godard's broader quest for cinematic 'truth' usefully focuses our attention on the relationship between filmic 'texts', historical narratives, and informational power structures both during and after the terminal crisis of the French over-

---

6. Leslie Hill, 'Filming Ghosts: French Cinema and the Algerian War', *Modern Fiction Studies*, 38, no.3 (Autumn 1992):787-804; p. 798 for the quotation.

seas empire. In order to make sense of that relationship, and thus of the French cinema's much-maligned response (or lack of it) to the Algerian War, it is useful to look briefly at the general role of cinema in the construction of French colonial myths, and then to go on to look more specifically at a key metaphor of French political and military failure in the Algerian context (together with its associated myth system): namely, the figure of the *'soldat perdu'* ('the lost soldier').

In fact, as Leslie Hill has pointed out, the single most striking feature of the French cinema's relationship with the territory is its long-term fascination with it as a privileged site for the acting out of European fantasies: 'In the late 1920s and 1930s, for instance, North Africa provided film-makers in France with a ready fund of familiar images of the exotic, mingling, for instance, the languid eroticism of Arabian nights with the infinite and hazy vistas of the Sahara to create a powerful confection of tragic heroism and passionate love'.[7] Such orientalist mythmaking served to reinforce the work done by the official propagandists of the French colonial enterprise, such as the *Agence Générale des Colonies* (AGC). As far as the use of film for overtly propagandist purposes was concerned, a leading role was played, unsurprisingly, by the *Service cinématographique de l'armée* (SCA). Recent research on this largely uncharted official production suggests that at least 316 propaganda films were made by the SCA during the Algerian war.[8] However, it is not this overt propaganda which will be considered here, but rather the contribution made to the French cinema's imaging of the Algerian conflict by the successors of such well-known colonial film-makers as Julien Duvivier and Jacques Feyder. More specifically, it is the role played by colonial myths and filmic metaphors that will interest us here, with particular reference to the figure of the *soldat perdu*, taken in this context to mean both seditious Right-wing officers (the standard usage) and forgotten conscript veterans of the war – together with the closely associated thematic of the confessional. For in what follows, it is the interrelationship of fragmented memories, multiple evasions, and belated filmic confessions which will be to the fore throughout.

The starting point for any discussion of the French cinema's response to the Algerian War must, inevitably, be to comment on

7. Hill, 'Filming Ghosts', p. 789.

8. Annette Vezin, 'Guerre d'Algérie, guerre de manipulation', *Le Monde*, 22/23 December 1996, p. 19.

the general absence of the war from French screens for the duration of the hostilities.[9] Even after Algeria's succession to independence, the first two films to depict the conflict directly were to be
foreign productions: Gillo Pontecorvo's masterpiece of agitprop,
La Bataille d'Alger (The Battle of Algiers) (1965) and Mark Robson's
Hollywood-produced *Lost Command* (1966). The most obvious reason for this absence was the strict censorship imposed by the
State, with the, previously noted, banning of Godard's modestly
critical *Le Petit Soldat* in 1960 serving to reinforce an established
mood of self-censorship among French film producers while the
war was still a 'live' issue. The post-1962 desire of the Gaullist
administration to turn the page rapidly and definitively on
France's colonial misadventures was itself systematically encouraged by the frenetic modernisation of the French society of the
day. If French film-makers as a body turned their backs on Algeria
after 1962, just as they had closed their eyes to it since 1954, they
were, perhaps, doing little more than reflecting the prevailing
national mood. In the wake of the upheavals of 1968, however,
producers and directors would return to the war as part of the
process of questioning which culminated in the new openness to
colonial history displayed in 1992 on the occasion of the thirtieth
anniversary of the Algerian cease-fire.

This said, Algeria was by no means as totally absent from
French screens between 1954 and 1962 as is often alleged. For one
thing, the activities of a leftist 'parallel cinema' ensured that oppositional shorts were both made and shown illegally, although
obviously to a very restricted – and already committed – audience
of anti-war militants. More generally, the war was made present in
many mainstream productions as a troubling mood of the times,
referred to by allusion or implication. So, for instance, both Jean-
Luc Godard's *A bout de souffle* (1960), the film which launched the
New Wave, and Louis Malle's stylish thriller *Ascenseur pour
l'échafaud* (Elevator to the Scaffold) (1957) have recently been (re)-
read as profoundly 'colonial' films.[10] However, such subtly allu-
sive references to the Algerian War are of interest precisely

9. Jean-Pierre Jeancolas talks of 'the strange silence of the French cinema regard-
ing decolonisation', *Le Cinéma des Français : La Cinquième République (1958-1978)*,
Paris, Stock, 1979, p. 156. Cf. Joseph Daniel, *Guerre et Cinéma*, Paris, Cahiers de la
Fondation Nationale des Sciences Politiques/Armand Colin, 1972, pp. 335-355.

10. Benjamin Stora, *La Gangrène et l'Oubli : La mémoire de la guerre d'Algérie*, Paris,
La Découverte, 1992, p. 40; David Nicholls, 'Louis Malle's *Ascenseur pour l'échafaud*
and the presence of colonial wars in French cinema', *French Cultural Studies* 7, part
3, no.21 (October 1996):271-82.

because of the absence of more direct representations of an eight-year-long conflict in which virtually an entire generation of young Frenchmen was obliged to serve.

In what follows, I shall seek to address the specificity of the French cinema of the Algerian War by revisiting two of its best known and most critically acclaimed productions: Alain Resnais's *Muriel* (1963) and Bertrand Tavernier's *La Guerre sans nom* (The War without a Name) (1992); together with two films on which critical opinion is much more sharply divided, Pierre Schoendoerffer's *Le Crabe-Tambour* (The Drummer-crab) (1977) and *L'Honneur d'un capitaine* (A Captain's Honour) (1982). For all their obvious differences – as regards the historical context in which they were produced and first consumed; their subject-matter and technical characteristics; and, above all, the overtly antagonistic political stances which they adopt – these works have much in common as regards both their most basic ideological assumptions and the rhetoric of their filmic reconstructions of the Algerian War. These similarities centre on the four films' common depiction of the war as an imperfectly suppressed (French) memory – a characterising feature of the French cinema of the Algerian War which has been condemned by Rachid Boudjedra among others[11] – and their similarly shared belief in the power of confession as both a psychological strategy and a filmic metaphor. For in all four works, the narration of individual guilt is presented as a model for the collective catharsis of the French nation. While these productions may be informed by a common belief in the power of on-screen confessions to heal psychological wounds, this notion gives rise in practice to radically different conceptions of the particularly fragmented and contradictory nature of 'History' in the Algerian context (and, perhaps, in all such wars of decolonisation, and the associated civil wars to which they have so often and so cruelly given rise). Such variations as a result reflect the extent of each film's engagement with the processes of historiography, including especially the need to take proper account of the profound, albeit depressing, need of modern nation-states to forget at least as much as they remember if they are to survive and thrive: the necessary escape from modern man's 'historical illness' first examined by Nietzsche. By extension, these films subscribe in rather different measures to the broad western myth of memory as

---

11. Rachid Boudjedra, *Naissance du cinéma algérien*, Paris, Maspero, 1971, p. 27. Cited by Stora, *La Gangrène et l'Oubli*, p. 41.

the possession of the individual rather than as a social construction – even in the work of Bertrand Tavernier, whose method of
filmic narration might seem on the surface precisely to emphasise
this social dimension – and to the more particularly French, and
specifically Proustian, myth of the nobility of the quest for the
recovery of 'lost memories', even if, as here, they are overwhelmingly of the bitterest kind.

We might usefully begin this reassessment by considering the
film which has been hailed by many critics – the present author
included – as epitomising the new French spirit of colonial openness that was prompted by, or at least coincided with, the thirtieth
anniversary of the ending of the Algerian War, Bertrand Tavernier's *La Guerre sans nom* (1992).[12] Consisting almost entirely of
interviews with a group of former conscripts from the Grenoble
region, Tavernier's film presents itself as an attempt to give a voice
to a group which has hitherto remained silent as regards its individual and collective experiences of Algeria. With the exception of
the opening and closing sequences, the authoritative voice-over
which we habitually associate with documentary is absent, with
the former soldiers being allowed rather to recount their personal
Algerian Wars in all their diversity. For the four hours or so that the
film lasts, the veterans are thus encouraged by Tavernier (through
his interviewer, Patrick Rotman) to remember things past, whether
mundane or extraordinary, pleasant or horrific, positively or negatively viewed. Generally interviewed alone – with both Algerians
and, with a single exception, women conspicuous by their absence
– the group of veterans respond to Rotman's basically gentle prob-
ing with only slightly varying degrees of openness. The treatment
accorded to the group is most straightforwardly confessional in its
handling of torture, where the complicity of a number of individuals is sympathetically explored, admitted, and, it would seem,
accepted. While some commentators have favourably compared
this technique with that used by Marcel Ophuls in his celebrated
exploration of the guilty secrets of the Occupation period, *Le Chagrin et la Pitié* (Sorrow and Pity) (1971), Leslie Hill has chosen to
subject Tavernier's approach to penetrating critical scrutiny. So,
whilst fully appreciating the undeniable strengths of Tavernier's
attempt to allow a forgotten group to express itself, he also draws
attention to the limitations of what he considers to be an essentially

12. Philip Dine, *Images of the Algerian War: French Fiction and Film, 1954-1992*,
Oxford, Clarendon Press, 1994, pp. 230-32.

formulaic 'story of restitution'.[13] Thus regarded, the film appears typical of Tavernier's *oeuvre*, particularly in so far as it reflects the director's determination to use the medium in order to engage in a form of 'narrative psychotherapy' which has been enthusiastically received by commentators both in France and further afield.[14] However, the conception of the relationship between film, memory, and history which underpins the film is a deeply problematic one, principally as a result of its failure at any stage to challenge the oral testimony provided by its ex-conscript witnesses by reference to other available forms of historical evidence. The end result, while undoubtedly highly charged in emotional terms, may nevertheless be judged reassuring as regards the French understanding of the Algerian War. In Leslie Hill's terms, '*La Guerre sans nom* ... functions ultimately more as an attempt to pacify conscience rather than to indict the past, more as an effort to enclose pain within narrative rather than to lend a voice to historical violence itself'.[15] To put the argument another way, it is as if the disparate narratives which, in the absence of a consensual history of the Algerian conflict, have competed for dominance of the French collective consciousness since 1962 are magically reconciled by Tavernier within a single, ultimately reassuring, meta-narrative.[16]

By way of a contrast, Hill looks to the fragmented narration of Alain Resnais's determinedly modernistic *Muriel* (1963) to demonstrate how a work of imagination, if sufficiently bold, may escape from the constraints of documentary as practised by Tavernier. A complex juxtaposition of stories, the film focuses most obviously on two overlapping wars and two overlapping male-female relationships: an older couple's love affair during the Second World War; and a recently returned conscript's involvement in the torture and murder of an Algerian woman, the 'Muriel' of the title. Another recent commentator on the film has noted that 'we have in *Muriel* a film whose most salient structural characteristics are generally seen to be fragmentation and de-centredness; and, of course, a film whose principal theme is that of torture'.[17] For Celia Britton, this relationship lies at the heart of the film and explains

13. Hill, 'Filming Ghosts', p. 790.

14. Ibid., p. 791.

15. Ibid., p. 792.

16. See Philip Dine, 'Reading and Remembering *la guerre des mythes*: French Literary Representations of the Algerian War', *Modern and Contemporary France*, 2/2 (1994):141-50.

17. Celia Britton, 'Broken Images in Resnais's *Muriel*', *French Cultural Studies*, 1, part 1, no.1 (February 1990):37-46 ; p. 38 for the quotation.

its abiding interest, in that it provides a formal and historical core which is, in fact, 'an *exploding* nucleus ... the structurally and metaphorically explosive secret of torture'.[18]

Britton's elegant and authoritative reading of *Muriel* relies for its coherence on the basic assumption that 'torture is the legacy of the Algerian War' and on the more specific observation that 'the only centre the film could be said to have is the unrepresented, in some sense absent, centre of the truth about the torture of Muriel'.[19] Leslie Hill sees the film in similar terms, and, indeed, bases his own high opinion of the work precisely on this self-conscious failure of representation. Hill's reading is supported by a sparkling critical deconstruction of this complex and multilayered work which privileges the functioning of the theme of torture as a 'metaphor for ... the political bankruptcy of Gaullist France, the bitter and unresolved contradiction between the France of the Liberation and the colonial France of the Algerian War'.[20] What is more, Hill argues, the film's preoccupation with the unspoken and the unspeakable actually reveals the limitations of political analysis itself in the Algerian context: 'It is to the failure of politics in the face of the resistance of Muriel's tortured body to meaning and narrative that, in the last analysis, Resnais and [screenwriter, Jean] Cayrol's *Muriel* bears witness'.[21]

However, there is perhaps an element of overstatement in Hill's assessment of the failure of representation involved here. After all, the primary historical significance of Resnais's film is that it was the first to break the cinematic taboo regarding the French army's use of torture in Algeria. Whatever either Britton or Hill may, with justice, say about the film's fragmentation, decentredness, and permanently unresolved silences, it is nevertheless true that at least one clear statement is made by Bernard, the returned conscript, and that this concerns the central ethical issue of the war for Metropolitan French intellectuals like Tavernier, namely the use of torture for the gathering of military intelligence. For Bernard undoubtedly confesses to the torture and murder of Muriel, with the result that the guilt of this 'soldier-citizen' becomes recuperable as a metaphor for the culpability of the whole French nation; as Hill himself recognises, for

---

18. Ibid., p. 40.
19. Ibid., pp. 40 & 38.
20. Hill, 'Filming Ghosts', p. 798.
21. Ibid., p. 803.

all his insistence on 'the powerful discontinuity which affects any representation of Muriel's death and makes its recovery problematic, if not in fact impossible'.[22] Bernard confesses to his Algerian crime, and in a way which is, if anything, less elliptical and thus more straightforwardly coherent than many other aspects of the film's narration.

Moreover, like that of Celia Britton, the highly sophisticated reading put forward by Leslie Hill ultimately depends for its force on the assumption that torture was the characterising feature of the Algerian War. This may pass without comment when viewed from a Metropolitan (and especially intellectual) French perspective, but has serious implications for the understanding of the Algerian War's historical specificity. At its most damaging, this reading of the conflict conceives of torture either as a metaphor for French colonial guilt as a whole or, more often, through a form of metonymy, reduces the complex history of Franco-Algerian hostilities simply to that aspect which had the greatest symbolic force for leftist and liberal intellectual observers (together with a limited number of Metropolitan participants). This is neither to deny the systematic use of torture and related pacification methods by the French army in Algeria, nor to question their inherently abhorrent nature. However, it is to set the ethical questions which such practices raised in the broader military and political context of the conflict, and thus to question the prevailing intellectual orthodoxies of the war years and since. For, as I have argued elsewhere, the Metropolitan intellectual preoccupation with military means served all too often to blind anti-torture campaigners to more basic political ends;[23] while the continued emphasis on the traumatised conscript's confession of torture – whether in Resnais's film in 1963, or Tavernier's in 1992 – encourages on the part of French audiences a sympathy with the plight of former national servicemen at the expense of other historical participants. Most obviously, these films permit no straightforward identification with the Algerian victims of French abuse, while sympathy for conscripted veterans may ultimately be arrived at only as a result of a compensating antipathy for the professional army in Algeria. Career officers (especially those in the often demonised parachute regiments) may thus be seen as primarily responsible for turning young

22. Ibid., p. 801.
23. Dine, *Images of the Algerian War*, pp. 64-88.

Frenchmen into an Algerian version of the Gestapo.[24] The result is a wilful confusion of the historical responsibilities of the makers and the executors of French colonial policy which has been encouraged by militant – if rather belated – leftist productions of the 1970s like René Vautier's *Avoir vingt ans dans les Aurès* (Twenty Years Old in the Aurès Mountains) (1972) and Yves Boisset's *RAS* (Nothing to Report) (1973). By way of a contrast, we may usefully consider two films which stand out from the leftist and liberal cinematic orthodoxy just mentioned in being the work of a rare Right-wing director who has regularly dared to speak his name.

Both *Le Crabe-Tambour* (1977) and *L'Honneur d'un capitaine* (1982) are typical of Pierre Schoendoerffer's literary and filmic *oeuvre* in their determination to make the case for the defence of the colonial officer corps, the single most maligned group of participants in the Algerian War. In both films, the painful reconstitution of the past is a structuring theme, with flashbacks constituting the primary mode of narration. Court cases are similarly central to both films, with the establishment of individual and collective responsibilities serving to encourage both the confession of personal sins and a reflection on national guilt. Although the films are quite different as regards their subject matter and mood, they may profitably be considered together.

Arguably Schoendoerffer's most accomplished film, *Le Crabe-Tambour* makes use of chronological layering to emphasise the continuities as well as the changes in the professional French military experience of the Second World War, Indochina, and Algeria. The principal point of view adopted is that of Pierre, a medical officer and Indo-China veteran, who plays a Marlowe-like role as the narrator of what is in places a self-consciously Conradian tale. However, the real focus of the film is to be found elsewhere, in the binary opposition of *le vieux* (the old man) and 'the drummer-crab', as the last voyage of a dying captain is used to trace the history of his relationship with a highly charismatic younger officer named Willsdorff. A larger-than-life figure whose adventures have taken him from Indo-China, via the South China seas and the Horn of Africa, to Algeria, Willsdorff will play a leading role in the attempted *putsch* of April 1961, in the course of which he extracts a commitment from his superior to join him in resigning his commission, whatever the outcome of the officers' revolt. The failure of 'the old man' to keep this promise will

24. See Philip Dine, 'The Inescapable Allusion: the Occupation and the Resistance in French Fiction and Film of the Algerian War' in H.R. Kedward and Nancy Wood (eds), *The Liberation of France: Image and Event*, Oxford, Berg, 1995, pp. 269-82.

result in his effectively being tried and convicted for dishonour by the court martial which almost incidentally sentences Willsdorff to twenty years in prison: a ritual humiliation of the older man which may well be at the root of the cancer that is eventually to claim his life. Set against the savage grandeur of the North Atlantic, this beautifully photographed, subtly juxtaposed, and finely acted film thus links the colonial past and the post-colonial present as 'the old man' makes one last voyage to say *adieu* – with no apologies, excuses, or forgiveness asked or expected on either side – to Willsdorff, now a humble fisherman on a Breton trawler. The Arctic pole of the French empire – represented by the islands of St Pierre and Miquelon and the Grand Banks of Newfoundland – thus acts as a counterpoint to the film's evocation of Southeast Asia and North Africa as, in the words of Jean-Pierre Jeancolas, the former comrades are finally 'reconciled in an atmosphere of noble death which pervades the whole film'.[25]

Military integrity and courtroom tension are even more obviously to the fore in *L'Honneur d'un capitaine*, in which Jacques Perrin, Schoendoerffer's *alter ego*, swaps his naval uniform for that of an army captain who is destined to lose his life in combat in Algeria. When, two decades later, in the course of a televised debate on the war, the dead soldier is denounced as a torturer and a murderer by a leftist sociology professor from the Sorbonne, his widow will seek to reconstitute her husband's past, previously a closed book to her, in an attempt to clear his name. At the heart of this particular colonial darkness are the dead officer's final days, which will be examined in detailed flashback in the course of the professor's trial for defamation, as will the French nation's collective conduct in Algeria. The complexity of the case, as of the war as a whole, is regularly emphasised as the doomed officer's last hours are recounted, against a backdrop of carefully observed locations and populations, and with little in the way of unproblematic heroism on any side.

The difficulty if not actually the impossibility of judgement at this geographical and historical remove is stressed as, in spite of the verdict given in his favour, real doubts remain about the dead officer's precise role in what were undoubtedly very unsavoury operations. It is made clear that, in Schoendoerffer's Algeria, mistakes, misunderstandings, and confusion have at least as important a part to play in the unfolding of events as conscious design, whether it be that of the dead captain or anyone else. As his widow's advocate puts it: 'We are dealing here with a tragedy. And

---

25. Jeancolas, *Le Cinéma des Français*, pp. 287-88.

in a tragedy the two adversaries have the same weight. The Algerian War was a tragedy. That is its grandeur. And also its horror.'

Tragedy, grandeur, horror, and a suspiciously convenient balancing of the forces of colonial repression against those of national self-determination: we are faced here with a fictive Algeria which has much in common with the Vietnam of Francis Ford Coppola. Indeed, like the American director's *Apocalypse Now* (1979), Schoendoerffer's visually stunning films are at least as informed by western myths of the Orient as they are by western military experiences of specific colonial conflicts.

Perhaps the most sustained critique of the account of French decolonisation presented in *Le Crabe-Tambour* is that offered by Naomi Greene. Drawing on Pierre Nora's theoretical reflections on historical memory, together with François de la Bretèque's insights into Schoendoerffer's mythic vision, Greene sets out to expose the mechanics of the film's undeniably nostalgic depiction of empire: 'an ambiguous world marked by the displacements and repetitions of dreams'. Thus regarded, *Le Crabe-Tambour* may, indeed, appear to be a work in which 'memory seeks less to recapture the past than to recreate it ... not to confront the ghosts of history but rather to establish a place where they may flourish forever'. However, to state, with justice, that the film functions as an 'archive' – that is, in Nora's sense, a repository for the self-serving memories of a particular interest group, in this case the colonial officer corps and their supporters – is not necessarily to prove that it constitutes an escape from France's colonial past rather than a contribution to its historical explication: 'a remembered world in which time has stopped and the past has absorbed the present'.[26]

While Greene's reading of *Le Crabe-Tambour* is both elegant and persuasive when the film is considered in isolation, her analysis becomes somewhat less convincing when the work is considered as just one half of Schoendoerffer's Algerian diptych. For if the earlier film seeks both to articulate and to celebrate the dream world of the colonial officer corps, *L'Honneur d'un capitaine* chooses instead to foreground the questioning of French military actions and motivations which began during the war years and

26. Naomi Greene, 'Empire as Myth and Memory' in Dina Sherzer (ed.), *Cinema, Colonialism, Postcolonialism: Perspectives from the French and Francophone World*, Austin, University of Texas Press, 1996, pp. 103-19; pp. 106 and 118 for the quotations; Pierre Nora (ed.), *Les Lieux de mémoire*, Paris, Gallimard, 1984; François de la Bretèque, 'L'Indochine au coeur d'une oeuvre: L'Iliade et l'Odyssée de Pierre Schoendoerffer', *Cahiers de la cinématèque*, no. 57 (October 1992).

has since been regularly reformulated. Of course, Schoendoerffer's second Algerian film also takes up where his first leaves off; most obviously by stressing the ambiguities of the French army's appointed mission in Algeria, and thus the officer corps's status as real – if very special – victims of French colonial adventurism. Predictably, this aspect of *L'Honneur d'un capitaine* has proved less than appealing to modern critics, who may themselves be prone to seek solace from historical complexities in a blanket denunciation of the colonial project's most devoted military agents. It is by no means impossible, in fact, that the contemporary critical desire to privilege what Greene calls 'the most troubling and "guilty" aspects of the colonial past – particularly the scandal at its heart, that is, the relationship between oppressed and oppressor'[27] may actually represent a retreat from even more troubling historical considerations, such as the collective responsibility of nations for the actions of their soldiers. As the counsel for the dead officer's accuser is forced to acknowledge: 'The really guilty parties are those politicians responsible for embroiling the French nation in an unjust war which could not but result in such excesses'. For, as John Talbott reminds us, French troops in Algeria 'were the executants of policy, not policy-makers'.[28] In short, the professional army's quest for collective integrity and individual authenticity in Algeria may often have been confused, even deluded, and self-serving, but it was no less real for all that. Viewed from this angle, the self-assured reaffirmation of activist military values to be found in *Le Crabe-Tambour* and *L'Honneur d'un capitaine* may be understood as the first stage in a cinematic de-dramatisation of the Algerian conflict. In Schoendoerffer's films, and in those less consciously oppositional works which followed it, the Algerian 'war of myths' becomes a setting, rather than a subject: an ideologically charged backdrop to the exploration of more universal themes, or a modern metaphor for tragic destiny, as the cultural historian Pascal Ory has aptly described it.[29]

By way of a conclusion, it is tempting to suggest that the Algerian 'lost soldier' has not so much been found again by the French cinema as periodically reconfigured according to the relevant filmmakers' preferred models of the history of French decolonisation.

27. Greene, 'Empire as Myth and Memory', p. 106.

28. John Talbott, 'The Myth and Reality of the Paratrooper in the Algerian War', *Armed Forces and Society*, 3 (Fall 1976):69-86; p. 78 for the quotation.

29. Pascal Ory, 'L'Algérie fait écran', in Jean-Pierre Rioux (ed.), *La Guerre d'Algérie et les Français*, Paris, Fayard, 1990, pp. 572-81; p. 579 for the quotation.

What we are still faced with, in fact, are competing myths of 'the war without a name' and, by extension, of the *'soldat perdu'*, each reflecting a distinct stage in the evolution of Metropolitan attitudes to the Algerian War: Alain Resnais in 1963 offered the conscripts' coded confessions, and a myth of the lost soldier as a New Wave antihero; Pierre Schoendoerffer in 1977 and 1982 presented the professional army's nostalgic confessions, and a myth of the lost soldier as a New Right antihero; while Bertrand Tavernier in 1992 put forward the veterans' documentary confessions, and a myth of the lost soldier as the troubled hero of France's newfound honesty as regards its colonial past. Thus, the French cinematic obsession with the voicing of individual guilt continues to hold sway: a limited perspective which may actually have hindered the nation's belated attempts to come to terms not only with its Algerian past, but also with its Algerian present and future. In a final irony, French film-makers and historians alike seem to suffer from a guilt complex inspired by the American cinema of the Vietnam war, which is regularly lauded as the model for western cinematic grappling with the sins of the colonial (or quasi-colonial) past.[30] A self-censorship rooted in the fear of artistic competition may thus have come to replace that which once sprang from the experience of government sanctions.

30. See, for instance, Stora, *La Gangrène et l'Oubli*, p. 255; cf. Jeancolas, *Le Cinéma des Français*, p. 156; and contrast Pierre Guibbert, 'La guerre d'Algérie sur les écrans français', in Laurent Gervereau, Jean-Pierre Rioux and Benjamin Stora (eds), *La France en guerre d'Algérie*, Paris, Collection du Musée d'Histoire Contemporaine – Bibliothèque de Documentation Internationale Contemporaine, 1992, pp. 247-55.

INDEX

A

A bout de souffle 146
Abd-el-Kader 143
Action Française 36
L'Action Française 75
Advertisements 7, 51, 59, 60, 83
Affari Politici Francia 69
Agence Générale des Colonies
   147
Albion, perfidious 12, 69, 70, 74,
   80
Algeria 1, 2, 9, 12, 126, 127, 129,
   136, 141, 142–157
Allies 1, 2, 24, 65, 66, 68, 72, 75,
   84, 93, 97, 98, 99, 104, 107, 112,
   113, 115; German allies 50,
   111, 114
Alsace-Lorraine 1, 118
Anglophobia 65–87
Anti-Semitism 55, 80, 116
Apocalypse Now 156
L'Appel 74
Arc de Triomphe 23, 44, 47
Arendt, Hannah 25
Aristocracy 135–138, 141
Armenians 22, 23
Armistice (WWI) 66
Armistice (WWII) 25, 47, 65, 78,
   79, 81, 93, 96, 97, 98, 103, 104,
   105, 109
Ascenseur pour l'échafaud 148
Atrocities/atrocity propaganda 6,
   16, 17, 18, 20, 24, 25, 53, 58, 114

Aubigny-en-Artois 25
Aujourd'hui 74
L'Aurore 60, 133
Avoir vingt ans dans les Aurès 154

B

La Baïonette 52
Bairnsfather, Bruce 64
Barrès, Maurice 45
Barthes, Roland 30, 68, 133
Bastille 27, 38, 39
La Bataille d'Alger 148
Battle of Algiers 145
Baudouin, Paul 71
BBC 65–87, 95, 112, 114
Bécassine 138
Becker, Annette 1, 6, 9, 12,
   (15–26)
Belgium 15, 83
Ben-Amos, Avner 12, (27–48)
Béraud, Henri 75, 76
Berthelot, Marcelin 42
Bhabha, Homi 142
Bloch, Marc 18
Blum, Léon 55
Boisset, Yves 154
Bolsheviks 12, 76, 100
Le Bonnet Rouge 54
Boudjedra, Rachid 149
Boulanger, General 42
Boulogne 66–68, 86, 87
Bretèque, François de la 156
Briand, Aristide 55

Britain 12, 25, 65–87, 97, 99, 103,
104, 106, 107, 128
Britannia monument 66–68, 85–86
Britton, Celia 151, 152, 153
Brunius, Jacques. 79
*Bulletin de l'Institut Français
d'Opinion Publique* 124
Burrin, Philippe 68, 69

C
Cagoule, Cagoulards 56
Calet, Henri 23
Le Canard Enchaîné 64
Candide 61
Cardinal, Roger 11, 14
Carlu, Jean 36, 59
Carnot, Sadi 42
Castries, General de 129, 133,
135, 136, 141
Cayrol, Jean 152
Centre National de la Ciné-
matographie 146
*Une Certaine Idée de la Résistance.
Défense de la France, 1940–1949*
122
Chack, Paul 74, 75, 76
Le Chagrin et la Pitié 150
Chateaubriand 112
Churchill, W. 71, 73, 97, 106
Cinq colonnes à la une 146
"Civilising mission" 1, 109, 141,
143, 144
Clandestine press 6, 17, 25,
111–125
Clemenceau, Georges 54, 72, 104,
107
Colin, Paul 59, 60, 63
Collaboration, Franco-German
62, 71, 73, 75, 76, 83, 84, 94, 97,
101, 103, 105, 107
Colonialism 1, 47, 127, 128, 131,
132, 133, 135, 136, 142–158
Combat 113–125
Concentration camps 16, 17, 114,
118
Confédération générale du tra-
vail (CGT) 28

Cooper, N. 9, 12, (126–141)
Coppola, Francis Ford 156
Cornick, M. 8, 12, 77, 78, (65–87)
Courrières, 25
Le Crabe-Tambour 149, 154, 156,
157
Crémieux-Brilhac, J.-L. 70, 83, 85
Crimes against humanity 20
Culture 3, 4, 5, 7, 9, 17, 22, 127,
142, 143, 157; culture of war,
17; folk culture, 3; revolution-
ary culture, 91

D
Dagen, Philippe 2
Dakar 12, 72, 73
Daladier 58
Dalimier, Albert 47
D'Angers, David 34
Darlan, Admiral 69, 75, 76, 81,
115
D'Astier 9
Daudet, Léon 54, 118
Déat, Marcel 76
Decolonisation 14, 148, 149, 156,
157,
Défense de la France 113, 114, 116,
117, 118, 121, 122
Degeyter, Pierre 48
Delavenay, Emile 77, 78, 81, 83,
85
Delporte, C. 4, 7, 12, (49–64)
Deportation 17, 22, 26, 118
Dien Bien Phu 12, 128–141
passim, 143, 145
Dietrich, Mayor of Strasbourg
33, 35
Dine, P. 9, 12, (142–158)
*Discours aux Français, 17 juin
1940–20 août 1944* 88–110
Discours et messages 88–110
Doriot 56, 81
Dreyfus Affair 4, 42, 50, 55, 75
Dunkirk 12, 49, 68, 72
Duquesne, Jacques 144
Duvivier, Julien 147
Dyssord, Jacques 51

E
Education 28, 35, 38, 47, 116, 117,
    127, 129
Embodiment 7, 9, 58, 71, 90, 129,
    132, 133, 134, 138, 140
Entente Cordiale 8, 66–71, 84, 86
L'Espionnage allemand à l'oeuvre
    51
L'Espionnage allemand en France,
    1914–1916 50
L'Espoir Français 75
Eugenics 19, 22

F
Fairy-tales 3
Faure, Christian 3
Ferdonnet, Paul 57, 72
Festival of Federation 39
Jacques Feyder 147
FFI (Forces Françaises de l'In-
    térieur) 99, 120, 124
Fiaux, Louis 46
Fifth Column 4, 9, 12, 49–64
Le Figaro 44, 54, 71, 131, 132, 134,
    136, 138
The First World War 68
Flood, C. 9, (88–110)
Foch 25, 107
Footitt, Hilary 96
For Whom the Bell Tolls 140
Forain 52, 54
Foreign Office, British 5, 55, 75
Franc-Tireur 114, 115, 118, 119,
    120, 122
France: Second Republic 39, 143
    Third Republic 27, 28, 34, 38,
    39, 41, 44, 70, 100, 105, 129,
    143
La France Libre 79
Franco–British relations 8, 12,
    65–87
Franco–German relations 5, 30,
    32, 73, 75, 76, 103
Front de Libération Nationale
    (FLN) 143, 144
Frye, Northrop 29, 31
Furet, François 28

G
Galard, Geneviève de 135,
    136–138, 140, 141
Gallus 79, 85
Gaulle, Charles de 2, 9, 62, 72, 73,
    85, 88–110, 146
Geneviève (St.) 9, 40, 140
George VI 66, 68
George-Edward 52, 53
German army 5
German Atrocities 24
German mythology 8
Germanophobia 19, 80, 118
Giap, General Vo Nguyen 130,
    131, 145
Giraudoux, Jean 56, 58, 75
Godard, Jean-Luc 146, 148
Goebbels 57
Golden Age 22, 135, 136
Gollancz, Victor 25
Gossec and Gardel 46
La Grande Illusion 63
Graves, Robert 8
Greek mythology 7, 8, 31
Greene, Naomi 156, 157
Grévy, Jules 39
Griffiths, Richard 89
Gringoire 55, 75
La Guerre sans nom 126, 149, 150,
    151
Guilt 12, 16, 18, 84, 99, 149, 150,
    152, 153, 154, 157, 158

H
Hague Convention 16
Hatred 25
Hemingway, Ernest 140
Heredity 19
Hill, Leslie 150, 151
Hirsch, David 18
Hirsch, Jean-Pierre 18
Hitler 5, 14, 22, 23, 24, 25, 60, 61,
    73, 80, 81, 84, 106, 113, 114,
    117, 119
Holocaust 6, 25, 26
L'Honneur d'un capitaine 149,
    154–157

Horne, John 17, 24, 26
Hostages 16, 17, 21
Hugo, Victor 28
L'Humanité 113, 115–119, 123

I
L'Illustration 43
Images d'Epinal 2, 3
Indochina (see also Vietnam) 1,
    2, 6, 9, 126–144, 154
Institut Français d'Opinion
    Publique 124
Invalides, Les 27–48
Internationale 38, 47, 48
Ireland 143

J
Jaurès, Jean 28, 116
Je Suis Partout 55
Jews 6, 25, 26, 55, 71, 76, 77, 80, 81
Joan of Arc 9, 70, 82, 101, 102,
    107, 108
Joantho, Louis de 46
Jouhaux, Léon 28

K
Kessel, Joseph 111
Kramer, Allan 24

L
La Rocque 56
Laval 12, 69, 70, 71, 81, 83
Leclerc, General 9, 107, 129
Legion of Honour 41
Lepeletier 41
Let My People Go 25
Liberation 62, 63, 75, 105, 152
Libération 113, 119, 120, 122
Ligue Anti-Britannique 74
Ligue des Patriotes 45
Lille 17, 19, 21, 22, 24
Lost Command 148
Louis XIV 32, 41, 107
Louis-Philippe 33, 34

M
La Madelon 46

Malle, Louis 148
Malvy, Jean-Louis 43, 44
Marat 41
Marengo 41
Marianne 9, 140
Marianne Into Battle 9
Marseillaise, The 27–48
Mass communication 2, 4, 5, 6;
    mass media, 14, 50
Mauriac, François 71
Maurras, Charles 75, 76, 100
McPhail, Helen 26
Memory and forgetting 3, 4, 7, 9,
    10, 11, 15, 16, 20, 21, 22, 23, 29,
    30, 45, 87, 126, 142, 149, 150,
    151, 156
Mendès-France, Pierre 143
Mers el Kébir 12, 68, 71, 72–73,
    74, 80
Metaphor 7, 10–14, 27, 29–31,
    138, 141, 142, 147, 149, 152,
    153, 157
Metonymy 29–30, 32, 44, 153
Millerand, Alexandre 51, 52, 56
Mirabeau 41
"la mission civilisatrice", see
    "civilising mission"
Mitterrand, François 143
Modernist art and literature 2, 3,
    151
Mosse, George 66, 67
Munich Accord 66, 67
Muriel 149, 151, 152, 153
Murphy, Robert 70
Mussolini 55, 106, 115
Myth 2, 4–12, 14, 15–17, 24, 26,
    27, 31, 34, 49, 50, 52, 55, 59–64,
    65–73, 77, 84, 85, 88–91, 94, 95,
    101, 103, 109, 110, 111, 112,
    123–125, 126, 129, 131,
    133–135, 140, 141, 142, 143,
    145, 149, 150, 156–159

N
Napoleon 32, 33, 37, 39, 41, 44,
    107, 119
Napoleon III 41

Nation and Narration 142
Nationalism 28, 35, 91, 106;
    Nationalists 28, 50, 55; Algerian, 144
Nazism 25, 71, 112, 113, 118; Nazi
    sympathisers 94
New Wave 146, 148, 158
Nietzsche, Friedrich 149
North Africa 2, 93, 135, 147, 155

O

Occupied France 1, 12, 16, 19–25,
    65–87, 88–110, 111–125, 150
Occupied Europe 6, 15, 23
Offering to Liberty 46
Oignies 25
Ophuls, Marcel 150
L'Opinion 52
Oran: see Mers el Kébir
Ory, Pascal 157

P

Pacifism 20, 21, 23, 24, 54, 64
Pantheon 28, 40–42, 47
Paris 2, 3, 9, 23, 33, 37, 39, 40, 44,
    45, 48, 52, 53, 58, 62, 67, 68, 74,
    75, 76, 78, 79, 84, 120, 124, 127,
    129, 140
Paris Commune 37, 142
Paris Match 128, 133, 135, 136,
    138, 145
Paris Metro 7, 51, 122
Pas-de-Calais 25, 79
Patriotism 19, 22, 33–48, 56, 62,
    78, 100, 101, 107, 117, 118, 124,
    132
Péguy, Charles 38
Le Pèlerin 57
Peterson, Ian 61
Pétain 2, 9, 62, 65, 68, 69, 70, 73,
    80, 81, 84, 85, 88–110, 111, 112,
    115, 123
Le Petit Soldat 146, 148
Phil 55
Phoney war 50, 55, 56, 57, 59, 70,
    79
Pils, Isidore 34, 35, 47

Poetics 11; poetic realism, 146
Poincaré, Raymond 40, 107, 132
Pollack, Michael 16
Pontecorvo, Gillo 148
Popular culture 2, 3, 5, 6, 29, 40,
    102, 136
Popular Front 47, 55, 70
Pottier, Eugène 48
Poulbot, Francisque 53, 54, 61
Propaganda 2, 4–7, 10, 11, 12, 13,
    14, 22, 24, 26, 30, 35, 50–64, 65,
    69–81, 102, 110, 111–125, 147
Protocols of Paris 75
Proust 150
Prussia 15, 28, 37, 38, 63
Psychiatry 19
Psychological warfare 7, 50, 64

R

R.A.S. 154
Radio Stuttgart 57, 59, 72
Race and racism 4 (note), 13, 19,
    132
Renoir, Jean 47
Resistance, French 2, 7, 9, 17, 25,
    62, 65, 81, 82, 84, 85, 94, 96, 99,
    102, 106, 111–120, 153–154
Résistance 113, 115, 118
Resnais, Alain 149, 151, 152, 153,
    158
Rethondes 25
Revolution, French 12, 27–48, 91,
    100, 108, 109, 142
Révolution Nationale 3 (note), 98,
    100, 102, 105, 108
Rhetoric 4, 10, 11, 12, 55, 104,
    132, 149
Ricoeur, Paul 10
Riom trials 100, 115
Ritual 31, 32, 42, 44, 94, 155
Rivière, Jacques 17
Robson, Mark 148
Romains, Jules 60
Rostand, Edmond 46
Rotman, Patrick 150
Rouget de Lisle, Joseph 27, 30,
    31, 32–36, 40, 42, 44, 45, 47, 48

Rousseau, Jean-Jacques 28, 41
Russia 15, 111, 112, 113, 119, 120,
    124, 129

S
Sacred Union 21, 43, 46, 47
Sarraut, Maurice 114
Schoendoerffer, Pierre 149,
    154–158
Serbia 15
Service cinématographique de
    l'armée 147
Shell shock 20
Socialism and socialists 20, 28,
    46, 47, 54, 99, 116, 120
S.S. 25
Strasbourg 32, 33, 34, 45, 47
Stroheim, Erich von 63

T
Talbott, John 157, 158
Tavernier, Bertrand 126, 149, 150,
    151, 152, 153, 158
Témoignage chrétien 116
Thermidorians 33, 41
Todorov, Tzvetan 3
Tonkin 12, 130, 131
Tourangeau, Roger 13
Trauma 1, 9, 12, 16, 18, 19, 20, 25,
    126, 141, 153
Treblinka 26
Turenne, Henri 41
Turmel, Louis 54

U
Underground press 111–125
United Kingdom 6 (see also
    "Britain")
United States 13, 70, 73, 106, 109,
    126, 145
Unknown Soldier 23, 47

V
Valmy 28, 37
Vautier, René 154
Verdun 12, 13, 57, 68, 92, 104,
    131, 132

Vichy 2, 3, 62, 65, 69, 70, 71, 73,
    75, 76, 77, 78, 80, 81, 93, 94, 96,
    100, 101, 103, 104, 105, 111,
    112, 114, 115, 116, 123, 125, 142
Vietnam (see also Indochina)
    126–141, 145, 156, 158
Viviani, René 43, 45
Voltaire 41

W
War: just 16
    of religion 17
    to end all wars 23
    unjust 157
Boer War 17, 70
Colonial wars 2, 9, 70, 126–158
First World War/Great War 1–6,
    9, 11, 12, 15–17, 21, 23–26,
    27–48, 50, 52, 55–57, 61, 63, 64,
    67, 72, 98, 104, 105, 115, 119,
    127, 131, 134, 135
Franco-Prussian War 1, 16, 25,
    32, 37
Second World War 2, 3, 5, 6, 9,
    15, 16, 22, 23, 25, 50, 99, 120,
    121, 136, 143, 151, 154
War Song for the Army of the Rhine
    29
Weber, Eugen 143
Wieviorka, O. 6, 11, (111–125)

Z
Zola, Emile 42

Index compiled by Helena Scott